TASTE LE
TOUR

TASTE LE
TOUR

Regional French Cuisine

GABRIEL GATÉ

ILLUSTRATED BY ANTONIA PESENTI

hardie grant books
MELBOURNE · LONDON

TABLE OF CONTENTS

Brest
BRITTANY
Quimper
Lori

Introduction	Page	vii
Soups, entrées & vegetables	Page	1
Fish & seafood	Page	29
Poultry & rabbit	Page	49
Beef, lamb & pork	Page	73
Cakes & desserts	Page	95
Index	Page	146
Acknowledgements	Page	151

Calais
Lille
Amiens
THE NORTH
bourg
Le Havre
Caen
ROUEN
ILE de FRANCE
Reims
LORRAINE
Strasbourg
NORMANDY
alo
Versailles
Paris
CHAMPAGNE
Nancy
Colmar
NES
THE LOIRE
Orléans
Chablis Dijon
FRANCHE -COMPTE
Angers
Tours
BURGUNDY and the LYONNAIS
Besançon and the ALPS
ntes
THE CENTRE
La Rochelle
Limoges
Vichy
Lyon
Cognac
Clermont- Ferrand
ANNECY
Bordeaux
Aurillac
GRENOBLE
Montélimar
THE SOUTHWEST
LANGUEDOC
Nimes
PROVENCE
Aix en Provence
Monaco
Nice
Toulouse
Montpellier
Marseille
ayONNE
THE PYRENEES and GASCONY
Pau Tarbes
Carcassonne
Perpignan

Published in 2010 by
Hardie Grant Books
85 High Street
Prahran, Victoria 3181, Australia
www.hardiegrant.com.au

Cataloguing-in-Publication data is available from the National Library of
Australia.
Taste Le Tour

ISBN 978 1 74066 892 7

Cover and text design by Michelle Mackintosh
Colour reproduction by Splitting Image Colour Studio
Printed and bound in China by C&C Offset Printing

INTRODUCTION

Each year in July millions of people all over the world enjoy watching the Tour de France bicycle race on television. Le Tour, as it is fondly called, is a marathon race of more than 3,500 gruelling kilometres across the stunning French countryside. It begins on the first Saturday of July, always from a different town – usually a French town but sometimes from outside France. Competitors cycle around France through at least a dozen different regions. The race always includes the challenging mountain roads of the Alps and the arduous Pyrenees and it finishes on the fourth Sunday of July with a wild sprint along the majestic Champs Elysées in Paris.

The broadcast of the Tour is a lot more than merely sporting coverage: it's a cultural experience. Day by day, via wonderful camera shots and expert commentary, viewers discover the beauty of France – its great history, stunning architecture and amazing agriculture – and delight in picturesque views of orchards, vineyards, pastures, grand homes, villages and much more.

I've been a fan of the race for many years, and since 2005 I have travelled to France to produce and present *Taste Le Tour*, a television segment, featuring the best of French gastronomy. It showcases the food, wine, cheese and special dishes of all the French regions that the cyclists pass through over the course of that year's race.

This cookbook is a collection of the delicious French dishes that were prepared for the show over the past five years. The recipes come from a handful of French chefs, in particular, Philippe Mouchel and myself, but also from local French pastry cooks and food artisans. Many of the dishes are easy to prepare, while others will challenge you.

Bon appétit and vive Le Tour!

CHAPTER ONE

SOUPS, ENTRÉES & VEGETABLES

YOUNG VEGETABLE SOUP

Potage aux primeurs
From Paris – Ile de France

The French adore soup and this sort of vegetable potage is extremely popular in the countryside around the Paris region, where many vegetables for the Parisian market are grown.

2 medium leeks
at least 1 cup celery leaves
   or 2 stalks of celery
½ cos lettuce
1 ½ litres chicken broth
   or chicken stock
1 cup shelled peas

2 tablespoons olive oil
1 tablespoon butter
2 slices bread, cut into 2 cm cubes
4 egg yolks
salt
freshly ground black pepper

Trim and wash the leeks and cut them into thin julienne strips, about 5 cm long.

Shred the celery leaves (or finely slice the stalks, if using). Wash and shred the lettuce leaves.

In a large saucepan, bring the chicken broth to the boil. Add the leeks, celery leaves, lettuce and peas and cook at a low boil for around 15 minutes, or until the vegetables are soft.

Meanwhile, heat the oil and butter in a frying pan and fry the bread cubes until lightly browned.

Place the egg yolks in a mixing bowl and whisk to combine. Slowly pour in about 1 cup of hot liquid from the soup, whisking continuously. Season with salt and pepper.

Pour the egg mixture into the soup (away from the heat), then season to taste. Ladle into deep soup bowls and serve the croutons separately.

Serves 4–6

MUSSEL AND SAFFRON SOUP

Soupe de moules au saffran

From the Languedoc Region by Philippe Mouchel

The French Mediterranean coast in the Languedoc region is dotted with wonderful little fishing villages where you can enjoy hearty, but delicately flavoured, seafood soups and stews in the local restaurants.

1 kg large very fresh mussels scrubbed and beards removed

2 shallots, finely sliced

½ onion, finely sliced

1 sprig thyme

1 bay leaf

a few parsley stalks

2 strips orange peel

250 ml dry white wine

3 diced tomatoes, peeled and seeded

1 tablespoon cornflour

2 tablespoons water

125 ml cream

a good pinch of saffron threads

30 g butter, cubed

freshly ground black pepper

4 tablespoons finely snipped chives

Place the mussels in a large saucepan and add the shallots and onion. Tie the thyme, bay leaf, parsley stalks and orange peel together with kitchen string and add to the pot. Pour in the wine and cover with a lid. Bring to the boil over a high heat and cook for a few minutes until the mussels have just opened.

Lift the mussels out of the cooking liquid and place in a bowl. Remove the onions and the herb bouquet. Taste the liquid and if it is too salty add a little water. Add the diced tomatoes and simmer for about 5 minutes. Meanwhile, remove the mussel meat from the shells and keep warm.

Mix the cornflour with the water then whisk into the simmering soup. Bring to the boil, then add the cream and cook for a few minutes. Add the saffron then blend in a liquidiser until smooth (or use a hand blender). Stir in the butter until melted then season with plenty of black pepper.

Divide the mussels between 4 soup plates, pour on a little of the soup and sprinkle with chives. Bon appétit!

Serves 4

MUSSELS COOKED WITH WHITE WINE AND HERBS

Moules marinières

From the Atlantic-Poitou Region by Philippe Mouchel

A survey done a few years ago showed that the average French person's favourite dish was moules marinières. The French consider it an affordable festive dish to be enjoyed on the terrace of a seaside restaurant during the long days of summer

2 tablespoons olive oil
2 shallots, finely sliced
1.5 kg mussels, thoroughly
   scrubbed and beards removed
100 ml dry white wine
a few sprigs parsley, plus
   2 tablespoons chopped parsley

1 bay leaf
2 sprigs thyme
freshly ground black pepper
50 g butter, cut into small pieces

Heat the olive oil in a large saucepan over a gentle heat. Add the shallots and cook, stirring continuously, for a few minutes. Add the mussels, white wine, parsley sprigs, bay leaf and thyme, and season with pepper. Cover with a lid and steam the mussels until they have all opened. It takes about 5 minutes. Shake the pan a couple of times during the cooking.

Lift the mussels out of the pan and place in a large serving bowl. Bring the mussel juices to the boil and boil for 2 minutes. Add the butter and stir until melted. Stir in the chopped parsley, pour the liquid over the mussels and serve at once.

Serves 2–3

FISH STEW

Bouillabaisse
From the Provence Region

This fish stew specialty of Marseille is traditionally made with a selection of rock fish. When well made it is one of my favourite French dishes. It is traditionally served with fried slices of baguette and a garlic mayonnaise.

2 tablespoons extra-virgin olive oil
1 onion, chopped
10 cumin seeds
20 fennel seeds
1 small red chilli, finely sliced
1 bulb fennel, cut into 8 wedges
1 kg tomatoes, peeled, seeded
    and chopped
1 litre fish stock

salt
freshly ground black pepper
a large pinch of saffron threads
2 kg firm white fish (flathead,
    gurnard, john dory), cleaned
    and heads removed
16 prawns, shelled and deveined
16 new potatoes, peeled and cooked
2 cloves garlic, chopped

Heat the oil in a casserole dish and heat gently. Add the onion, cumin seeds, fennel seeds and chilli and fry for 1 minute. Add the fennel pieces and fry for 1 minute. Add the tomatoes and stir for 1 minute. Add the fish stock and season with salt, pepper and saffron. Bring to the boil, then boil for 10 minutes.

Add the whole fish to the casserole dish and simmer for 10 minutes. Add the prawns and simmer for a further 5 minutes.

Transfer the fish and vegetables to a platter and garnish with boiled potatoes.

Stir the garlic into the cooking liquid and transfer to a soup tureen.

Diners serve themselves by placing the seafood and potato into deep soup plates and ladling the liquid over the top.

Serves 8

Note: French people love fish, and to obtain the maximum flavour, they always cook fish on the bone when making bouillabaisse. Then as they eat it, they patiently remove the bones from the flesh.

MARINATED SARDINES

Sardines à l'escabèche
From the Provence Region

This traditional dish of sardines, marinated with vinegar, oil and herbs, is often associated with the historic Mediterranean Provençal city of Marseille. Marseille is famous for its daily fish market where sardines and other seafood are sold just hours after the catch.

12 fresh medium sardines
3 tablespoons lemon olive oil,
 plus a little extra for drizzling
salt
freshly ground black pepper
½ medium onion, very finely sliced
1 medium baby carrot, finely sliced
1 teaspoon coriander seeds

1 bay leaf
4 sprigs thyme
2 cloves garlic, unpeeled
60 ml good quality white
 vinegar (I use champagne
 vinegar)
125 ml cold water

Clean the insides of the sardines, scale them and cut off the heads. Dry the sardines with kitchen paper.

Heat 2 tablespoons of the lemon olive oil in a large frying pan and fry the sardines for 1–2 minutes on each side. Be careful not to overcook them. Season the sardines with salt and pepper and arrange them on a flat platter.

Heat the remaining lemon olive oil in a separate frying pan. Add the onion, carrot, coriander seeds, bay leaf, thyme and garlic cloves and cook gently for 2 minutes. Add the vinegar and water, bring to the boil and simmer for 15 minutes.

Spoon the hot liquid, herbs and vegetables over the sardines. Allow to cool, cover with plastic film and refrigerate for 24 hours. The sardines will absorb the liquid.

Just before serving, drizzle the sardines with a little extra lemon olive oil.

Serves 4 as an entrée

CRAYFISH AND POTATO SALAD

Salade de langouste aux pommes de terre.
From the Atlantic Island Region by Philippe Mouchel

*The Atlantic coast south of the Loire River is dotted with many islands, one of which
is Noirmoutier, which is famous for its shellfish and new-season potatoes.
As a boy I enjoyed several summer holidays in Noirmoutier.*

1 x 800 g cooked crayfish
2–4 small new potatoes,
   cooked in their skins
120 g green beans, cooked, but firm
2 tomatoes, peeled, quartered
   and seeded
a few green salad leaves

juice of 1 lemon
sea salt
freshly ground black pepper
4 tablespoons olive oil
2 tablespoons finely snipped
   chives

Remove the crayfish from the shell and cut the tail meat into slices just less than
1 cm thick.

Peel and slice the potatoes.

Arrange the crayfish and potato slices attractively on 2 plates. Garnish with a
little bouquet of green beans and a few tomato quarters. Top with green salad
leaves.

To make the dressing, whisk the lemon juice with a little salt and pepper then
whisk in the olive oil. Add the chives and drizzle the dressing over the salad.

Garnish with extra fresh herbs if you wish, then serve.

Serves 2

CRAYFISH À LA PARISIENNE

Langouste à la Parisienne

From the Paris Region by Philippe Mouchel

During my younger days I worked in a wonderful Parisian seafood restaurant called Prunier where I learned to prepare this classic dish of crayfish with a diced vegetable and mayonnaise salad. This is Philippe's recipe and to present the dish he uses 10 cm PVC rings.

3 tablespoons diced turnips, about 6 mm square
3 tablespoons diced carrots, about 6 mm square
3 tablespoons diced beans, about 6 mm square
3 tablespoons diced potatoes, about 6 mm square
2 tablespoons shelled peas
1 egg yolk

2 tablespoons mustard
salt
freshly ground black pepper
2 teaspoons vinegar
freshly ground black pepper
100 ml olive oil, plus a little extra for drizzling
1 x 400 g cooked crayfish
a few cos lettuce leaves
a few chives for garnishing

Cook the turnips, carrots, beans, potatoes and peas separately in boiling salted water (either use separate saucepans or change the water for each vegetable). Drain each vegetable well then place on a tea towel to absorb any excess water.

In a bowl, mix the egg yolk with the mustard, a little salt and pepper and the vinegar. Gradually pour in the olive oil, whisking continuously, until you obtain a thick mayonnaise.

Place the cooked, drained vegetables in a bowl and mix with half the mayonnaise.

Remove the crayfish tail meat and cut into 1 cm slices.

To serve, place a PVC ring in the centre of each plate. Spoon in the vegetable mix to about 1 ½ cm and flatten the surface with a spoon. Arrange a few overlapping slices of crayfish on top of the vegetables and carefully remove the PVC rings. Top with a few lettuce leaves and a small dollop of mayonnaise.

Drizzle on a little extra olive oil, sprinkle with a few chives and serve.

Serves 3

COUNTRY-STYLE PÂTÉ WITH PISTACHIOS

Pâté de campagne à la pistache

From the Burgundy Region by Stéphane Langlois

Burgundy is one of the great gastronomic regions of France with its superb wines and meat, and, of course, wonderful cuisine. Also popular is the charcuterie (smallgoods), such as this festive country-style paté which used to be made on the farm and served for special occasions.

750 g lean pork leg meat, cubed
350 g pork fat, cubed
550 g chicken livers, cleaned
  and trimmed
a handful of parsley leaves
½ brown onion, roughly chopped
40 g salt (or less, to taste)
1 teaspoon ground white pepper
1 teaspoon mixed spices
1 tablespoon chopped garlic

2 teaspoons dried thyme
60 ml Cognac or brandy
2 tablespoons cornflour
2 medium eggs
120 g shelled pistachios
a few strips of thinly cut pork
  fat, optional
10 g gelatine
300 ml warm water

Preheat the oven to 90°C. Grease a 2-litre terrine dish.

Mix together the pork, pork fat, chicken livers, parsley and onion. Put the mixture through a mincer then transfer to a bowl and stir in the salt, white pepper, mixed spices, garlic and dried thyme. Add the Cognac, cornflour, eggs and pistachio nuts and mix everything together thoroughly.

Tip the paté mixture into the terrine dish and smooth the top. Decorate with a few strips of the thinly cut pork fat arranged in a criss-cross pattern.

Place the terrine in a baking dish and pour in hot water to a depth of about 4–5 cm to create a bain-marie. Bake in the preheated oven for about 3 hours. When it is cooked, the temperature of the terrine will have reached 80°C at its centre.

Remove the terrine from the oven and stand on a cool surface. Dissolve the gelatine in the warm water and pour over the terrine. Allow the terrine to cool, then refrigerate until ready to serve.

Slice the terrine while still in the dish and serve with gherkins and French bread.

Serves 12

POTATO GALETTES WITH A WALNUT AND ROQUEFORT CHEESE SALAD

Galettes de pomme de terre, salade de roquefort aux noix
From the Languedoc Region

This dish is so French – and so typical of the northern part of Languedoc, not far from where the famous roquefort blue cheese is made. The use of duck fat to cook the potatoes is essential for the authentic flavour. It is available from specialist butchers and good delicatessens.

1 clove garlic, finely chopped
salt
freshly ground pepper
1 tablespoon red wine vinegar
3 tablespoons olive oil
2 cups of mixed green leaves

60 g roquefort cheese,
   broken into small pieces
4 shelled walnuts, very
   roughly chopped
2 medium potatoes, peeled
2 tablespoons chopped parsley
2 tablespoons duck fat

Place half the garlic in a large mixing bowl with a little salt and pepper and the vinegar and whisk together well. Whisk in the oil gradually. Add the green leaves, cheese and walnuts to the bowl and toss everything together gently.

Grate the potatoes onto a plate and pat dry with kitchen paper. Tip into a bowl with the remaining garlic and the chopped parsley. Season with salt and pepper and mix well.

Heat the duck fat in a 20 cm frying pan. When the fat is hot add the potato mixture to the pan to form a large galette around 1 cm thick. Press with the back of a spoon or fork to flatten and cook for a few minutes. Carefully turn the galette over and cook the other side (to turn the galette, slide it onto a plate, then turn the plate over and slide the galette back into the pan.

Cut the cooked galette in half or quarters and divide between 2 plates.
Serve with the dressed salad.

Serves 2

ROSCOVITE SALAD WITH CAULIFLOWER AND PRAWNS

Salade Roscovite

From the Brittany Region by Philippe Mouchel

This classic Breton salad was named after the coastal town of Roscoff in Brittany. The locals adore cauliflower which is just as important as the prawns in this lovely salad. For an elegant presentation, use 10 cm PVC rings.

¼ cauliflower,
  cut into medium florets
12 cm piece of cucumber,
  cut into cubes
2 potatoes, cooked
  in their skins and cubed
1 egg yolk
1 teaspoon Dijon mustard
salt
freshly ground pepper

1 lemon
125 ml extra-virgin olive oil,
  plus 2 tablespoons extra
3 tablespoons cream
3 tablespoons chervil leaves
3 tablespoons tarragon leaves
16 cooked prawns, peeled
  and deveined
4 hard-boiled eggs, quartered

Cook the cauliflower florets in boiling salted water for a few minutes, until just tender. Drain and cool in cold water. Drain again and cut into smaller pieces.

Place the cauliflower, cucumber and potato in a bowl.

In a second bowl make a mayonnaise by whisking the egg yolk with the mustard, a little salt and pepper and a few drops of lemon juice. Slowly drizzle in 125 ml of olive oil, whisking continuously until thick and creamy. Whisk in the cream and set aside.

Roughly chop two-thirds of the chervil and tarragon leaves, reserving the rest for garnish. Add to the vegetables and toss with the extra 2 tablespoons of olive oil.

Carefully spread 2 tablespoons of the creamy mayonnaise over each of the 4 plates. Place a PVC ring in the centre and spoon a few tablespoons of the vegetable salad into the rings. Lift the ring away carefully.

Divide the prawns and hard-boiled eggs between the plates, arranging them attractively around the vegetable salad. Scatter with the reserved chervil and tarragon on top and serve.

Serves 4

ASPARAGUS AND GOAT'S CHEESE TART

Tarte aux asperges et au fromage de chèvre
From the Loire Valley Region by Philippe Mouchel

The sandy soil of the Loire Valley produces superb asparagus and almost every restaurant in the region serves an asparagus dish in the two or three months leading up to the Tour de France.

400 g rolled puff pastry
2 egg yolks,
1 teaspoon water
16 thin green asparagus spears,
 trimmed

2 tablespoons cream
salt
freshly ground pepper
80 g fresh goat's cheese

Preheat the oven to 170°C. Line a flat baking sheet with baking paper.

Cut the rolled pastry into a rectangle about 10 x 30 cm and place on the baking sheet. Using the blade of a knife, lightly mark a 1 cm border down the long sides of the rectangle. Weight down the centre of the pastry (use baking paper with rice or small pastry weights) to stop it from rising during the cooking.

Lightly beat one of the egg yolks with the water to make eggwash and use to brush along the pastry edges. Bake for 15–20 minutes, or until the edges have risen and are golden brown.

Drop the asparagus spears into lightly salted boiling water for 2–3 minutes, then drain well.

Remove the baking paper and weights from the pastry. Lightly beat the remaining egg yolk with the cream and brush over the centre of the pastry. Season with salt and pepper. Top neatly with the cooked asparagus and spoon any remaining egg yolk and cream over the top. Dot with small pieces of goat's cheese and season with a little more salt and pepper. Return to the oven and bake for around 5 minutes, until the cheese is warm and lightly browned. Cut in half before serving.

Serves 2

YABBIES IN PUFF PASTRY

Ecrevisses en chausson

From the Alps Region by Philippe Mouchel

Yabbies are very popular in France and are found on the menus of the best French restaurants, especially around the Alps region where there are lots of freshwater streams.

2 rectangles rolled puff pastry,
   12 cm x 8 cm x 3 mm thick
1 egg yolk
2 teaspoons cold water
6 cm piece carrot
6 cm piece leek
6 cm piece celery
1 teaspoon olive oil
2 tablespoons butter

2 tablespoons cream
½ tablespoon
   finely chopped tarragon
½ tablespoon finely
   chopped parsley
6 thin slices truffle
12 cooked yabbies, shelled
salt
freshly ground black pepper

Preheat the oven to 180°C. Line a flat baking sheet with baking paper.

Place the puff pastry rectangles on the prepared baking sheet. Using the tip of a knife, lightly mark a smaller rectangle inside each pastry rectangle, forming a 5 mm border.

Mix the egg yolk and water together to make eggwash and brush over the pastry. Bake for 15–18 minutes, or until lightly browned and risen. It should rise at least 2 cm if the pastry is good quality.

Cut the carrot, leek and celery into thin slices and then into thin julienne strips. Heat the oil and butter in a small saucepan over a medium heat. Add the vegetables and cook for a few minutes until soft. Add the cream, tarragon and parsley, then add the truffle slices and yabbies and reheat. Season to taste.

Cut the smaller rectangle out of the cooked puff pastry, and set this 'lid' aside. Remove any excess pastry from the centre to create a cavity. Spoon in the yabby and vegetable mixture, replace the pastry lids and serve straight away.

Serves 2

GRATIN OF YABBIES

Gratin d'ecrevisses

From the Alps Region by Philippe Mouchel

This stunning dish used to be served in many of the top three-star restaurants all over France. It's fairly rich but is a real classic and a great dish to learn and to serve for special occasions.

1.5 kg cooked yabbies
4 tablespoons olive oil
40 g butter
3 shallots, finely sliced
1 fennel stalk
1 tablespoon tomato paste
1 tomato, diced
60 ml Cognac
125 ml Madeira
125 ml white wine,
   plus 2 tablespoons extra
500 ml crayfish or fish stock

1 bay leaf
2 sprigs thyme
80 ml thin cream
a pinch of cayenne pepper
2 egg yolks
100 g warm melted butter
juice of ¼ lemon
2 cups cooked spinach
1 clove garlic, chopped
salt
freshly ground black pepper

Detach the yabby heads from the bodies and shell the yabby tails.

Heat 2 tablespoons of the olive oil in a heavy, cast-iron saucepan. When very hot, add the yabby heads and stir well for a couple of minutes, pressing on the heads from time to time to extract more flavour.

Add half the butter to the pan then add the shallots and fennel and stir well. Add the tomato paste and stir well. Stir in the diced tomato, Cognac, Madeira and white wine and bring to the boil. Add the crayfish stock, bay leaf and thyme and simmer for 20 minutes, uncovered. Stir in the cream and cayenne pepper and cook for a further 5 minutes.

Strain the yabby sauce through a chinois or very fine sieve into a saucepan, pressing on the shells to extract the maximum flavour. Simmer the sauce over a medium heat until reduced to about 1 ½ cups.

Place the egg yolks and the 2 extra tablespoons of white wine in a medium bowl and sit it over a saucepan of simmering water. Whisk the yolks over the heat for about 5 minutes until they are light and fluffy. Remove the bowl from the saucepan and gradually add the melted butter, whisking continuously to form a creamy sauce. Whisk in the lemon juice

Melt a teaspoon of the remaining butter in a saucepan. Add the cooked spinach and garlic and warm through gently.

Melt the rest of the butter and the remaining 2 tablespoons of oil in a pan and gently reheat the yabby tails. Season to taste with salt and pepper and gently stir in the yabby sauce.

Arrange the spinach in a 25 cm gratin dish. Top with the yabbies and sauce and place under a hot grill until lightly browned on top. Serve immediately.

Serves 4

MUSSEL GRATIN WITH SPINACH

Moules gratinées aux epinards

From the North Coast Region by Philippe Mouchel

This mussel dish is out of this world, and so French, with the flavour of garlic butter.

1 tablespoon olive oil
120 g butter
1 shallot, finely chopped
20 mussels in their shells,
    thoroughly scrubbed and
    beards removed
10 parsley stalks, plus
    3 tablespoons chopped parsley

50 ml dry white wine
2 cloves garlic, chopped
juice of ½ lemon
salt
freshly ground black pepper
200 g baby spinach leaves
60 ml cream
3 tablespoons dried breadcrumbs

Heat the olive oil and 1 teaspoon of butter in a large saucepan. Stir in the chopped shallot and cook for 2 minutes. Add the mussels, parsley stalks and white wine to the pan. Cover with a lid and cook for a few minutes until the mussels have just opened.

Place the rest of the butter in a small bowl, keeping 1 teaspoon in reserve. Add the chopped garlic, chopped parsley, lemon juice and a little salt and pepper.

Heat the remaining teaspoon of butter in a large saucepan and cook the spinach until wilted. Drain well.

Heat the cream in a small saucepan and when it boils, stir in the wilted spinach.

Remove the mussel meat from the shells. Arrange 20 half shells on a large plate or serving dish. Spoon a little of the creamed spinach into each shell and top with a mussel. Spoon a little herbed butter onto each mussel, then sprinkle lightly with breadcrumbs. Place under a hot grill for a few minutes until the breadcrumbs are lightly browned. Serve immediately.

Serves 2

BUCKWHEAT PANCAKES FROM BRITTANY

Galettes Bretonnes au Sarazin

From the Brittany Region by Jean-Marie Blanchot

These savoury buckwheat pancakes are the pride of Brittany's cuisine and I am very fond of them myself. They're usually prepared on special circular hot plates about 30 cm in diameter, but at home you can use a very large non-stick frying pan.

250 ml cold water
½ teaspoon salt
200 g buckwheat flour
10 g salted butter, melted,
    plus extra unmelted butter for
    greasing the pan and to rub on
    top of the pancakes

4 eggs
120 g grated gruyère cheese
4–8 thin slices of ham

Place most of the cold water and the salt in a large bowl and mix well. Add the flour and whisk to a smooth batter. It should fall like a ribbon when you lift the whisk. If necessary, add a little extra water.

Mix in the melted butter until well incorporated. Cover the batter and rest in the fridge for about 4 hours.

When ready to cook the pancakes, lightly grease a large non-stick frying pan and heat over a medium flame. Pour in enough of the batter to cover the base very thinly. When the underside of the pancake is dry, lower the heat and rub the surface of the pancake with a piece of extra butter.

Break an egg in the centre and spread the white all over the pancake, keeping the yolk intact. Sprinkle with grated cheese and top with a slice or two of ham.

Using a spatula, carefully fold the sides of the pancake in towards the yolk to form a square. Cook for an extra minute or two, then transfer to a warm plate while you make the rest of the pancakes.

Serves 4 as an entrée

CHEESE SOUFFLÉ

Soufflé au fromage
From the Jura Region

The Jura mountain range bordering the Franche Compté and Switzerland, produces really flavoursome cheeses with lovely melting qualities. They are used frequently by local cooks in recipes such as this delicious soufflé.

30 g butter
30 g plain flour
350 ml milk
¼ teaspoon freshly
   grated nutmeg
a good pinch of cayenne pepper

freshly ground black pepper
2 small egg yolks
50 g grated gruyère cheese
50 g grated emmental cheese
6 egg whites
a pinch of cream of tartar

Preheat the oven to 180°C. Butter and flour an 18 cm soufflé mould.

Melt the butter in a saucepan over a medium heat. Whisk in the flour and cook for about 2 minutes. Slowly add the milk, whisking constantly until it forms a smooth white sauce. Cook gently for 3–4 minutes, then turn off the heat.

Mix in the nutmeg, cayenne pepper and a little black pepper. Then add the egg yolks and grated cheese and mix in well. Transfer the soufflé base to a large bowl.

Whisk the egg whites with the cream of tartar until stiff. Mix a little of the beaten whites into the soufflé base to loosen the mixture, then gently fold in the remaining whites.

Pour the soufflé mixture into the prepared soufflé mould and smooth the surface. If you wish, you can decorate the surface with small, flat, diamond-shaped pieces of cheese for effect.

Bake for about 35 minutes, then serve immediately. Take care when carrying the hot soufflé to the table. To serve, spoon the soufflé onto plates.

Serves 4 as an entrée

FRENCH-STYLE ONION AND ANCHOVY PIZZA

Pissaladière.

From the Provence – Côte d'Azur Region by Philippe Mouchel

The sunny Côte d'Azur on the coastal region of France next to Italy is typified by this Pissaladière, a flavoursome French-style pizza much loved as a snack or as an appetiser served with drinks.

50 g butter

3 large brown onions,
  very finely sliced

500 g ready-to-use bread dough,
  or a large ready-to-use pizza base

3 tablespoons extra-virgin olive oil

20 anchovy fillets, drained of oil

25 black olives, pitted

25 small sprigs of thyme,
  about 1 cm long

freshly ground black pepper

a little plain flour to
  dust the bench

Preheat oven to 190°C. Line a baking sheet with baking paper.

Heat the butter in a large, non-stick frying pan. Add the onions and cook on a low heat for about 20 minutes, stirring from time to time. Don't try to cook the onions too fast or they will burn and taste unpleasant. Allow the onions to cool slightly before using.

Roll the bread dough out to a thickness of about 5 mm and carefully lift it onto the prepared baking sheet. Brush with a little of the extra-virgin olive oil.

Spread the cooked onions on top of the dough, leaving a margin of about 2 cm at the edges. Decorate with the anchovy fillets, making a criss-cross pattern. Arrange the olives and sprigs of thyme in the spaces between the anchovies and season with a little black pepper.

Bake for about 15 minutes or until the pastry is brown and crisp and it smells wonderful. Cut into pieces and serve.

Serves 6–8 as an appetiser with pre-dinner drinks

QUICHE LORRAINE

From the Lorraine Region by Philippe Mouchel

This is perhaps the best known French dish outside France and can be easily varied by using different cheese, spices and herbs. It's a very traditional dish.

Pastry

125 g butter, cut into pieces

1 egg yolk

a pinch of salt

2 cups plain flour

3 tablespoons water

juice of ½ lemon

Filling

2 egg yolks

2 whole eggs

100 ml milk

300 ml cream

salt

finely ground black pepper

2 pinches freshly grated nutmeg

1 teaspoon butter

100 g bacon, diced

100 g grated gruyère cheese (or another cheese of your choice)

To make the pastry, place the butter, egg yolk, and salt in a food processor and blend to combine. Add the flour, water and lemon juice and blend to form a ball. Remove from the food processor, wrap in plastic film and refrigerate for at least 30 minutes before using.

Preheat the oven to 230°C. Grease and line a 22 cm loose-bottomed flan tin.

Roll out the pastry on a floured surface and use to line the flan tin. Trim the edges and line the pastry with a sheet of foil. Fill with pastry weights, (or use rice or dried beans). Cook for about 12 minutes, then carefully remove the foil and weights.

In a bowl, whisk together the yolks, eggs, milk and cream. Season to taste with salt, pepper and freshly grated nutmeg.

Lower the oven temperature to 180°C.

Melt the butter in a frying pan and cook the bacon for 3 minutes, turning occasionally. Drain the bacon well then scatter over the par-cooked pastry shell. Sprinkle on the cheese then pour in the egg mixture.

Carefully transfer the quiche to the oven and cook for 20–25 minutes, or until the filling is set and the top is golden brown. When cooked, remove from the oven and leave for about 10 minutes before unmoulding.

Serves 6

SILVERBEET GRATIN

Gratin de blettes
From the Alps Region

Many French people eat their main meal of the day at lunchtime, then for dinner they often have a satisfying vegetarian dish such as this lovely silverbeet gratin, an Alpine speciality that uses flavoursome local cheese.

8 silverbeet leaves with
the stalks, well washed
60 g butter
salt
freshly ground pepper
¼ teaspoon grated nutmeg
120 ml cream

20 g plain flour
300 ml milk
a pinch of cayenne pepper
around ½ cup finely
grated gruyère cheese
3 tablespoons dried breadcrumbs

Trim the leaves from the silverbeet stalks. Cut the stalks into 3 cm pieces and shred the leaves.

Heat a third of the butter in a saucepan. Add the silverbeet stalks and stir for 3 minutes over a medium heat. Season with salt and pepper, cover with water and cook for about 15 minutes, or until soft. Drain well and set aside.

Heat another third of the butter in a different saucepan. Add the shredded silverbeet leaves and cook until wilted. Season with nutmeg, a little salt and pepper and half the cream. Set aside.

Melt the rest of the butter in a saucepan over a medium heat. Whisk in the flour and cook for 1 minute. Slowly add the milk, whisking constantly until it forms a smooth white sauce. Season with cayenne pepper, stir in the remaining cream and simmer for 2 minutes. Add the drained silverbeet stalks and mix in about 2 tablespoons of the gruyère cheese.

Spoon the cooked silverbeet leaves into a 25 cm gratin dish. Pour on the white sauce, then scatter on the remaining cheese and top with the breadcrumbs. Place under a hot grill until lightly browned. Be careful when serving, it's very hot!

Serves 3–4

PROVENÇAL VEGETABLE BAKE

Tian aux légumes Provençals
From the Provence Region

*This excellent Provençal vegetable dish is typical of the region and a good example of
how creative the Mediterraneans are with their vegetables.*
*'Tian' is actually the name of the cooking dish used. You will need a large ovenproof
dish, made of either porcelain or cast-iron.*

125 ml extra-virgin olive oil
1 large brown onion, finely sliced
1 red or green capsicum, seeds
   removed and finely sliced
2 medium eggplants,
   halved and finely sliced
1 clove garlic, finely chopped
4 medium zucchinis

6 tomatoes, cut into 5 mm slices
salt
freshly ground black pepper
2 tablespoons finely chopped
   lemon thyme
2 tablespoons grated parmesan
3 tablespoons dried breadcrumbs

Heat half the olive oil in a large, non-stick frying pan. Add the sliced onion and
cook, stirring continuously, for 2 minutes. Add the capsicum and cook for
2 minutes, stirring again. Add the eggplant and garlic and cook over a low heat
for about 20 minutes, or until the vegetables are soft.

Preheat the oven to 160°C.

Using a vegetable peeler, peel off the zucchini skin in vertical strips, 1 cm apart,
so that strips of skin remain. Cut the zucchinis into 5 mm slices.

Transfer the cooked vegetables to an ovenproof dish. Arrange the zucchini and
tomato slices on top of the vegetables in alternate, overlapping rows. Season with
salt and pepper and sprinkle evenly with lemon thyme. Drizzle evenly with the
remaining olive oil.

Bake for about 30 minutes. Sprinkle with parmesan and breadcrumbs and bake
for a further 10 minutes.

Serves 6

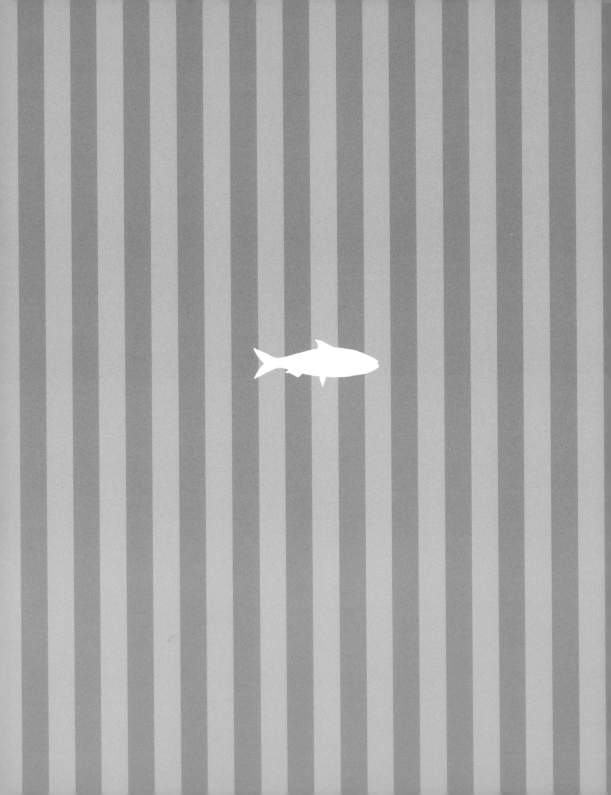

CHAPTER TWO

✤

FISH &
SEAFOOD

SCALLOPS THE PARISIAN WAY

Coquilles St Jacques à la Parisienne
From the Paris Region by Philippe Mouchel

The French are very fond of scallops and this delicate dish is a popular family favourite for Sunday lunch. If you have the chance to visit Paris, go to one of the many produce markets and admire the outstanding fish available. This dish looks lovely when presented on empty, clean scallop shells.

12 fresh scallops, cleaned and briefly rinsed	1 egg yolk
8 mushrooms, sliced	½ lemon
250 ml strong fish stock	salt
20 g butter	freshly ground pepper
20 g plain flour	60 g finely grated gruyère cheese
4 tablespoons cream	2 tablespoons dried breadcrumbs

Place the scallops in a saucepan with the mushrooms. Add the stock, and place over a medium heat. Bring to a low simmer and cook for 20 seconds. Drain the scallops and mushrooms, reserve and cool the stock. Divide the scallops and mushrooms between 4 clean scallop shells and set aside.

Melt the butter in a small saucepan over a medium heat. Whisk in the flour and cook for 2 minutes. Slowly add the cool stock, whisking constantly until it thickens to form a sauce. Stir in 2 tablespoons of cream and cook for a further 2 minutes.

In a small bowl, mix the egg yolk with the rest of the cream. Remove the sauce from heat and whisk in the cream and egg mixture. Add the lemon juice and season with salt and pepper.

Spoon some sauce over the scallops and mushrooms in the shells. Sprinkle with a little grated gruyére and breadcrumbs. Place under a hot grill until golden brown. (Alternatively, you can place the shells in a hot oven.) Serve immediately.

Serves 4

RED MULLET WITH TAPENADE AND A FENNEL SALAD

Filets de rouget poêlé à la tapenade, salade de fenouil

From the Provence Region by Philippe Mouchel

Red mullet is a really tasty fish and greatly loved by gourmets. It goes well with strongly flavoured ingredients such as olives, anchovies and fennel. I love it.

80 g black olives, pitted
1 teaspoon capers
3 anchovy fillets
4 tablespoons olive oil
1 clove garlic, finely chopped
3 basil leaves, finely chopped,
 plus 3 whole leaves
juice of 1 lemon

1 bulb baby fennel, trimmed
 and finely sliced
¼ red onion, finely sliced
4 cherry tomatoes, quartered
2 sprigs fennel leaves, chopped
 (or use dill)
salt
freshly ground black pepper
6 fillets red mullet

To make the tapenade, combine the black olives, capers and anchovy fillets in a small food processor and blend to a paste. Continue blending while adding 1 ½ tablespoons of the olive oil. Transfer the paste to a bowl and stir in the garlic, chopped basil and the juice of a little less than half a lemon. Set aside.

Place the fennel, red onion and cherry tomatoes in a bowl. Roughly tear the 3 whole basil leaves and add them to the bowl with the chopped fennel leaves. Season with a little salt and pepper, 1 tablespoon of olive oil and the juice of ½ lemon. Mix well and put aside.

Heat the remaining tablespoon of olive oil in a non-stick frying pan over a medium–high heat and cook the red mullet fillets, skin side down, for 2 minutes. Turn the fish and cook for 10 seconds.

Divide the salad between 2 plates. Arrange 3 fish fillets on each salad and top with a little tapenade. Serve straight away.

Serves 2

FISH QUENELLES

Quenelles de poisson

From the Lyonnais Region by Philippe Mouchel

Philippe Mouchel, talented chef and my good friend, learned to make fish quenelles when he worked with the world famous French chef, Paul Bocuse, in Lyon. This is Philippe's classic and delicious recipe. The quenelles have a unique texture and a wonderful crayfish flavour.

250 ml milk

75 g butter

4 egg yolks

125 g plain flour

250 g delicate white
   fish fillets (john dory, flathead)

1 egg white

100 g veal kidney fat,
   cut into very small pieces
   (available from good butchers)

a pinch of nutmeg

salt

freshly ground pepper

400 ml crayfish bisque
   (make your own or buy a can)

100 g crayfish meat,
   cut into small pieces

Bring the milk and butter to the boil in a medium saucepan.

In a bowl, mix the egg yolks with the plain flour. Add to the milk and whisk until it thickens and forms a mass (called a 'panade'). Transfer the panade to a bowl to cool.

Place the fish and egg white in a food processor and blend to a purée. Add the veal kidney fat and pulse briefly. Add the cool panade gradually, pulsing to incorporate, then season with nutmeg, salt and pepper. Transfer to a bowl and refrigerate for at least 1 hour.

Bring a large wide saucepan of water to a very gentle simmer. Using two large oval spoons, carefully mould some of the mixture into the traditional quenelle shape (practice makes perfect!). You should get between 6–8 quenelles from the mixture. Place the quenelles in the hot water to poach for 6–8 minutes, then drain on absorbent paper.

Preheat the oven to 200°C. Gently heat the crayfish bisque.

Transfer the quenelles to several small ovenproof dishes – aim for 2 quenelles per person. Spoon in the crayfish bisque, so it comes three-quarters of the way up the quenelles, and garnish with a little crayfish meat. Bake for 10 minutes, then serve.

Serves 3–4

CRAYFISH À L'ARMORICAINE

Langouste à l'Armoricaine

From the Brittany Region by Elisabeth Kerdelhué

This classic Breton crayfish dish was on the menu of many of the finest French restaurants at the end of last century. For me, when prepared by a master chef, it remains one of the greatest classic French dishes.
The prawn stock can be made ahead of time. This recipe makes around 500 ml and it keeps well in the freezer.

Prawn Stock
2 tablespoons olive oil
prawn shells from
   20 medium prawns
750 mls cold water
3 sprigs parsley
salt
freshly ground black pepper

1 sprig thyme
a few sprigs parsley
½ bay leaf
2 tablespoons olive oil
1 x 1 kg uncooked crayfish,
   cut into 8 pieces
2 shallots, chopped

1 clove garlic, chopped
20 ml Cognac
100 ml dry white wine
250 ml prawn stock
   (or use a good strong fish stock)
2 tomatoes, diced
1 teaspoon tomato paste
a pinch of cayenne pepper
2 tablespoons cream
1 tablespoon butter
1 tablespoon tarragon leaves,
   finely chopped
salt
freshly ground black pepper

To make the prawn stock, heat the oil in a saucepan and stir-fry the prawn shells over a high heat for 3–4 minutes. Add the water, parsley and a little salt and pepper. Return to the boil and simmer for 15 minutes, stirring occasionally.

Strain the stock through a sieve, pressing on the prawn shells to extract as much flavour as possible. Set aside until ready to use.

Use kitchen string to tie the thyme, parsley and bay leaf together to make a bouquet garni.

Heat the olive oil in a heavy saucepan. Add the crayfish pieces and sauté for 1 minute. Turn them over and sauté for a further 1–2 minutes, or until the shells have turned red. Remove the crayfish pieces from the pan.

Add the shallots and garlic to the pan and stir over a medium heat for a couple of minutes. Return the crayfish pieces to the pan and stir well. Add the Cognac to the pan and carefully flame it. (It is safest to do this away from the stove.) Add the wine, fish stock, tomatoes, bouquet garni, tomato paste and cayenne to the pan and stir gently. Cover and simmer for 10 minutes.

Transfer the crayfish pieces to a serving dish and keep warm.

Pour the sauce and any pieces of shell into a strainer set over a saucepan and press down to extract the juices. Stir in the cream and butter and reheat gently. Just before serving, add the tarragon and season with salt and pepper.

Spoon the sauce over the crayfish and serve. It's lovely served with boiled potatoes.

Serves 2

CRAYFISH STEW

Civet de langouste

From the coast of Languedoc-Roussillon Region by Philippe Mouchel

This special crayfish stew has a real taste of the Mediterranean region, especially when made using Banyuls, a local fortified wine that is very popular as an aperitif.

4 tablespoons extra-virgin olive oil
½ brown onion, chopped
3 tomatoes, peeled, seeded,
    and diced
1 clove garlic, chopped
1 bay leaf
4 sprigs parsley
1 x 500 g crayfish tail in
    the shell, cut into 6 pieces

salt
freshly ground pepper
20 g butter
10 ml Cognac
80 ml Banyuls
a pinch of cayenne pepper
4 thin slices prosciutto-style
    ham, roughly torn
a few sprigs chervil

Heat 1 tablespoon of the olive oil in a non-stick saucepan. Add the onion and cook over a medium heat for a few minutes. Add the tomatoes, garlic, bay leaf and parsley, then cover the pan and cook over a low heat for 30 minutes.

Season the crayfish pieces with a little salt and pepper.

Heat 2 more tablespoons of olive oil in a frying pan and cook the crayfish pieces on all sides for a few minutes. Add the butter and when it has melted, baste the crayfish. Add the Cognac, bring to the boil and flame. Add the Banyuls, bring to the boil and flame again. When flaming, it is safest to remove the pan from the stove. Remove the crayfish pieces from the pan, then boil the liquid until reduced by half.

Add the tomato mixture to the pan and season with cayenne pepper, salt and pepper. Bring to a simmer, return the crayfish pieces to the pan and simmer in the sauce for a few minutes.

Add a few pieces of ham to the sauce and warm gently. Spoon a little sauce onto two plates and divide the crayfish pieces between them. Top each serve with a few pieces of ham, drizzle on the remaining olive oil and garnish with chervil.

Serves 2

RICH BASQUE FISH STEW

Ttoro

From the Basque/Atlantic Region

Basque cooking is influenced by both French and Spanish cuisine. It is full of colour and strong flavours, such as olive oil, chilli and saffron.

1.5 kg firm, whole, white fish,
  (flathead, gurnard)
4 tablespoons olive oil
1 small leek, finely sliced
1 small onion, finely sliced
½ small capsicum, diced
½ long red chilli, finely sliced
2 tomatoes, finely diced
1 clove garlic, crushed
1 sprig thyme
2 sprigs parsley

a pinch of saffron threads
150 ml dry white wine
salt
freshly ground black pepper
50 g plain flour
12 scampi
500 g mussels, thoroughly
  scrubbed and beards removed
4 tablespoons chopped parsley
4 slices toasted bread,
  rubbed with raw garlic

Ask your fishmonger to clean and scale the fish, and to cut it into 5 cm pieces. Ask him to remove the fish heads and to cut them into pieces.

Heat 2 tablespoons of the oil in a large saucepan. Add the leeks, onions and fish heads. Cook over a medium heat for 5 minutes, stirring occasionally.

Add the capsicum, chilli, tomatoes, garlic, thyme, parsley and saffron and stir well. Add the wine and bring to the boil. Add enough water to cover and season with a little salt and pepper. Bring to a simmer and cook for 30 minutes, uncovered.

Pat the fish pieces dry and coat lightly with flour.

Heat the remaining 2 tablespoons of oil in a large saucepan and fry the fish pieces for about 1 minute on each side. Add the scampi, then the mussels. Strain the fish stock into the pan, shake well and cover with a lid. Cook over a medium heat until the mussels have opened.

Ladle the stew into deep soup plates. Sprinkle with chopped parsley and serve with the garlic toasts.

Serves 6

TROUT WITH PINE NUTS AND CAPERS

Truite Grenobloise

From The Alps Region by Philippe Mouchel

I cooked this beautiful trout dish hundreds of times when I was a young chef working in Paris. It's very easy to do at home.

4 tablespoons oil

2 slices bread,
  cut into 1 cm cubes

2 fresh trout, thoroughly
  cleaned, inside and out

salt

freshly ground black pepper

3 tablespoons plain flour

80 g butter

3 tablespoons pine nuts

3 tablespoons capers

1 lemon, peeled and cut
  into segments

juice of ½ lemon

3 tablespoons chopped
  parsley

Heat half the oil in a frying pan and fry the bread cubes until golden. Drain on kitchen paper.

Season the fish with salt and pepper and dust all over with a little flour.

Heat the remaining oil in a clean frying pan and cook the fish for 4 minutes on each side. Add one-third of the butter to the pan and baste the fish. Transfer the fish to a serving plate and keep warm.

Add the remaining butter to the pan. Stir in the pine nuts and cook for 1 minute until golden brown. Add the capers, lemon segments and lemon juice and reheat. Add the chopped parsley and spoon the sauce over the trout. Scatter the croutons on top and serve.

Serves 2

ROAST SNAPPER WITH MONTPELLIER BUTTER

Daurade rôtie au beurre de Montpellier

From the Languedoc Region

The sunny city of Montpellier in southern France is a lovely place to visit. There's a great tradition in the region of blending the seafood with the produce of the land. Montpellier butter is a very tasty accompaniment and goes well with fish.

1 x 1 kg snapper, scaled and cleaned	**Montpellier Butter**
sea salt	50 g butter, softened
freshly ground black pepper	1 tablespoon chopped parsley
3 tablespoons olive oil	1 tablespoon chopped chervil
2 shallots, finely sliced	6 tarragon leaves, finely sliced
2 teaspoons fennel seeds	1 small gherkin, finely chopped
4 sprigs parsley	6 capers, finely chopped
80 ml dry white wine	1 anchovy fillet, finely chopped
	juice of ¼ lemon
	freshly ground black pepper

To make the Montpellier butter, place the softened butter in a bowl and add the chopped parsley, chervil, tarragon, gherkin, capers, anchovy, lemon juice and a little freshly ground black pepper. Mix with a fork until just combined. Scrape this herb butter onto a piece of foil, roll up into a neat log and refrigerate until firm.

Preheat the oven to 200°C.

Make several 1 cm deep cuts in the thickest part of both sides of the fish and season with sea salt and pepper.

Pour half the oil in a baking dish large enough to hold the snapper. Scatter half the shallots, half the fennel seeds and the 4 parsley sprigs on the base of the dish. Place the snapper on top and scatter on the remaining shallots and fennel seeds. Drizzle the wine and remaining oil over the fish, cover with foil and bake for 25 minutes.

To serve, discard the parsley stalks and carefully lift the snapper flesh away from the bones. Serve with a slice of Montpellier butter. It's lovely with a tomato salad.

Serves 2

PERCH FILLET WITH ASPARAGUS AND CHABLIS SAUCE

Filet de perche sauce au Chablis et aux asperges
Burgundy Region

If you are a food and wine lover, Burgundy is one of the top regions of France to visit, and Chablis is a most charming village nestled amongst the chardonnay vineyards.

50 g butter
1 shallot, finely chopped
2 button mushrooms, finely sliced
2 x 200 g fillets perch
salt

freshly ground black pepper
50 ml chablis (chardonnay wine)
6 fat asparagus tips
2 tablespoons cream
4 sprigs of chervil

Melt a quarter of the butter in a frying pan over a medium heat. Add the shallot and stir for 30 seconds. Add the mushrooms. Top with the fish fillets, season with salt and pepper and pour the wine around the fish.

Cover the pan with foil or a lid and steam over a low heat until just done. It only takes 6–8 minutes.

Meanwhile, steam the asparagus tips until tender.

Transfer the fish and mushrooms to a serving dish or 2 plates and cover with foil. Bring the cooking liquid to the boil and cook for 2 minutes. Whisk in the remaining butter. When it has all melted, add the asparagus tips to the sauce.

Top the fish with the asparagus and spoon on the sauce. Garnish with chervil sprigs and serve.

Serves 2

PAN-FRIED SALMON WITH BUTTER SAUCE

Saumon poelé au beurre blanc

From the Loire Valley Region by Philippe Mouchel

Beurre blanc was the star sauce during my apprenticeship in the Loire Valley and chef Albert Augereau was a master at preparing it. This classic sauce has become less popular because of its butter content but it's so delicious! The reduction part of the sauce may be made ahead of time, but the cream and butter should not be added until you are ready to serve as the sauce does not reheat well.

2 medium potatoes, peeled
10 asparagus spears, trimmed
1 tablespoon vegetable oil
2 salmon cutlets
10 g butter
salt
freshly ground black pepper

Beurre Blanc Sauce
1 large shallot or ½ medium
  white onion, finely chopped
60 ml dry white vinegar
60 ml dry white wine
1 teaspoon cracked pepper
1 teaspoon cream
100 g very cold butter,
  cut into small cubes

To make the beurre blanc sauce, start by combining the shallots, vinegar, white wine and pepper in a small saucepan. Bring to a simmer and cook for 5–10 minutes, or until almost all the liquid has evaporated. Set aside.

Steam the potatoes and asparagus separately, until tender.

Meanwhile, heat the oil in a frying pan and cook the salmon cutlets for 2 minutes on each side. Add the butter to the pan and baste the salmon. Season with salt and pepper.

While the salmon is cooking, gently reheat the shallot reduction. Add the cream and bring to the boil. Lower the heat to a minimum and whisk in the butter, piece by piece. During this time the sauce must be whisked constantly. It should hold together and be creamy and smooth.

Arrange the salmon on 2 plates with the asparagus and potatoes. Serve the sauce either on the side of the plate or separately in a sauce boat.

Serves 2

BLUE EYE AND SCALLOPS WITH BUTTER SAUCE

Cabillaud et coquilles St Jacques au beurre blanc
From the Brittany/Loire Valley Regions

The west of France, with the Channel and the Atlantic Ocean, has a wonderful repertoire of excellent fish dishes. I am a native of Western France and when I was young my mother usually preferred to serve a fish dish such as this for special occasions rather than a meat dish.

60 g butter, cut into cubes
1 shallot, finely chopped
2 tablespoons white wine vinegar
5 tablespoons dry white wine
freshly ground black pepper
1 zucchini

2 fillets blue eye, skinned
200 g fresh scallops, cleaned
salt
1 teaspoon cream
a sprig of dill

Melt 1 teaspoon of the butter in a small saucepan over a low heat. Add the chopped shallot and stir for 1 minute. Add the vinegar and 3 tablespoons of the white wine, season with black pepper and simmer until the liquid has nearly all evaporated. Set aside

Cut the zucchini into thin slices, and then into thin julienne strips.

Melt another teaspoon of the butter in a saucepan over a medium heat. Add the zucchini julienne and stir for 20 seconds. Add the fish fillets to the pan, cook for 1 minute, then add the scallops. Season with salt and pepper. Add the remaining white wine, cover with foil and cook over a low heat for around 2 minutes. Turn the fish over and cook for a further 2 minutes.

Add the cream to the shallot mixture. Place the pan on a low heat and slowly whisk in the remaining butter, cube by cube, until melted and smooth.

Place the fish fillets on two warm plates. Top with a little zucchini, then a few scallops. Spoon on some of the butter sauce, garnish with dill and serve.

Serves 2

JOHN DORY WITH A CREAMY SEAFOOD SAUCE

St. Pierre sauce Normande

From the Normandy Region by Philippe Mouchel

The cold waters of the English Channel are ideal for producing delicate fish and seafood and most coastal towns and villages of Normandy have one or several excellent seafood restaurants.

12 mussels, thoroughly
  scrubbed and beards removed

50 ml white wine

10 g butter

2 shallots, finely chopped

150 g mushrooms

2 small john dory, gutted,
  skinned and heads removed

250 ml fish stock

salt

freshly ground black pepper

2 slices lemon

a few parsley stalks

4 medium uncooked prawns,
  shelled and deveined

4 large oysters

1 egg yolk

50 ml cream

juice of ¼ lemon

2 tablespoons chopped parsley

Place the mussels in a saucepan with the white wine. Cover with a lid and cook over a high heat for a few minutes until the mussels have opened. Remove the mussel meat from the shells and set aside. Strain the cooking juices into a bowl.

Place the butter, shallots, mushrooms, fish, mussel juices and fish stock in a wide saucepan or frying pan and season with salt and pepper. Place the lemon slices on the fish and add the parsley stalks to the pan. Bring to a very slow simmer, cover with a lid and poach for 5 minutes. Turn the fish over and simmer for another few minutes. Carefully lift the fish onto a warm plate and cover with foil.

Transfer the mushrooms to a separate saucepan with a few tablespoons of the cooking liquid. (Set aside the pan with the remaining cooking liquid). Add the prawns, oysters and mussels to the mushrooms. Cover the pan with a lid and steam over a high heat for 1 minute.

Return the pan with the reserved cooking liquid to the heat and boil until reduced by half.

In a small bowl, whisk together the egg yolk and cream. Pour into the reduced liquid, whisking continuously, until it thickens slightly. It is best to do this away from the heat.

Strain the sauce into the cooked seafood and mushrooms. Add the lemon juice and season to taste. Spoon over the fish, sprinkle with chopped parsley and serve.

Serves 2

POACHED TROUT WITH HOLLANDAISE SAUCE

Truite au bleu hollandaise

From The Alps Region by Philippe Mouchel

The beautiful streams and lakes in the Alps region are teeming with trout, so it has become the specialty of the area. The French often prefer their fish poached rather than pan-fried or deep-fried.

3 litres cold water
1 onion, thinly sliced
1 carrot, thinly sliced
a few parsley stalks
1 bay leaf
2 sprigs thyme
10 peppercorns
2 very fresh river trout (not rainbow
    trout), thoroughly cleaned,
    inside and out

½ cup parsley leaves
60 ml white vinegar

Hollandaise Sauce
80 g butter
1 egg yolk
2 teaspoons hot water
salt
freshly ground black pepper
1 teaspoon lemon juice

Place the cold water in a large pan over medium heat and add the onion and carrot. Use kitchen string to tie the parsley stalks, bay leaf and thyme sprigs together to make a bouquet garni and add to the pan with the peppercorns. Bring to the boil and cook for 10 minutes.

Meanwhile, make the hollandaise sauce. Melt the butter in a small saucepan over a low heat until warm, but not hot. Combine the egg yolk and hot water in a bowl set over a saucepan of hot water. Season with a little salt and pepper and whisk for a few minutes until light and fluffy. Remove the bowl from the heat, then very slowly add the warm melted butter, whisking continuously until well incorporated. Stir in the lemon juice.

Carefully place the trout in the hot poaching liquid and heat until close to boiling point. Poach the fish for 10 minutes. Turn off the heat, add the parsley and leave to stand for 3 minutes.

Heat the vinegar in a small saucepan. Carefully lift the two trout onto a flat dish and spoon on the hot vinegar, which gives them a blueish tinge.

Arrange the trout in deep serving plates with some of the vegetables and 2–3 tablespoons of the cooking liquid. Drizzle on a little hollandaise sauce and serve the remaining sauce in a small bowl on the side.

Serves 2

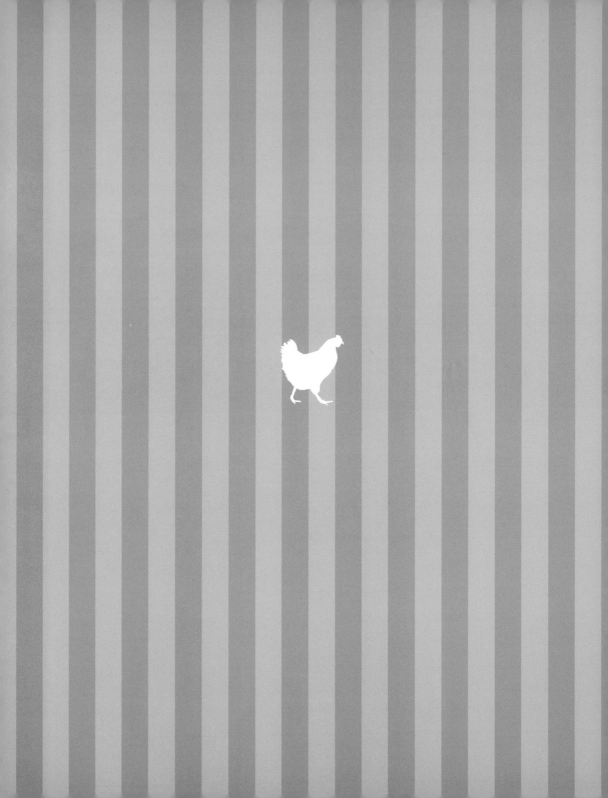

CHAPTER THREE

POULTRY
& RABBIT

SAUTÉED CHICKEN WITH TARRAGON CREAM SAUCE AND CARROTS

Poulet sauté à la crème d'estragon et aux carottes
From the Lyon/Central France Region

One of the highlights of French cooking is its wonderful variety of poultry dishes. Chicken with tarragon is so French and is often served as a main course at Sunday lunch for the extended family.

1 tablespoon extra-virgin olive oil
8 pieces chicken on the bone
   (thighs or drumsticks)
2 shallots, finely chopped
60 ml dry white wine
5 medium carrots,
   peeled and thinly sliced

20 g butter
60 ml water
salt
freshly ground pepper
60 ml thickened cream
3 tablespoons tarragon
   leaves

Heat the olive oil in a wide, non-stick saucepan and brown the chicken pieces on all sides. Add the shallots, then stir and cook over a low heat for 5 minutes. Add the wine to the pan and bring to a simmer. Cover with foil and a lid and cook over a low heat for about 20 minutes.

Meanwhile, place the carrots in a saucepan with the butter and water and season with salt and pepper. Cover the pan and cook for about 10 minutes, or until the carrots are tender.

When ready to serve, add the cream to the chicken and bring to a simmer uncovered, turning the chicken pieces around in the sauce. Stir in 2 tablespoons of the tarragon leaves.

Divide the carrots between four plates and top each with two pieces of chicken. Spoon a little sauce over the top, garnish with the remaining tarragon leaves and serve.

Serves 4

ROAST POUSSIN WITH FRENCH LENTILS

Poussin rôti aux lentilles du Puy

From the Centre of France/Massif Central Region

The delicious and delicate green lentils from the town of Le Puy-en-Velay are world-famous and loved by all, from the most humble cook to the top French chefs.

2 poussins (baby chickens)
2 tablespoons olive oil
2 sprigs thyme, finely chopped
freshly ground black pepper

French Lentils
10 g butter
30 g bacon, cut into small pieces
¼ onion, finely chopped
2 sprigs thyme

a few sprigs parsley
½ bay leaf
½ carrot, diced
3 tablespoons diced celery
¾ cup Puy lentils
1 clove garlic, whole
375 ml chicken stock
salt
freshly ground black pepper
3 tablespoons chopped parsley

To prepare the lentils, heat the oil and butter in a saucepan. Add the bacon and fry for 1 minute. Add the onion, stir well and fry for 1 minute.

Use kitchen string to tie the thyme, parsley and bay leaf together to make a bouquet garni.

Add the carrot and celery to the pan and stir well. Add the bouquet garni, lentils and garlic. Add the stock and bring to a simmer. Cover with a lid and cook over a low heat for about 40 minutes, or until the lentils are tender.

The lentils may be prepared ahead of time and gently reheated. Season with salt and pepper and stir in the chopped parsley just before serving.

Rub the poussins all over with 2 tablespoons of the olive oil and the chopped thyme. Season with pepper, cover and refrigerate until 10 minutes before cooking.

Preheat the oven to 160°C.

Place the poussins in a small oven tray and roast for about 35 minutes, turning the birds a couple of times during the cooking. Rest for 10 minutes before carving and serve with the lentils.

Serves 2–4

BRESSE CHICKEN WITH MOREL MUSHROOMS

Poulet de Bresse aux morilles

From the Franche Compté Region – East of Lyon

The chickens from around the town of Bourg-en-Bresse are considered by many to be the finest in France for flavour and texture. Select the best quality chicken you can find for this dish. Dried morels are readily available from good supermarkets and delicatessens. They need to be rinsed and soaked before using. Fresh morels are usually fairly clean, but brush away any visible dirt.

10 g dried morels or
   100 g fresh morels
10 baby carrots, peeled
20 g butter
2 corn-fed chicken breast fillets
salt
freshly ground black pepper

1 shallot, finely chopped
50 ml strong veal stock
2 tablespoons cream
2 tablespoons chopped
parsley
juice of ¼ lemon

Preheat the oven to 130°C.

If using dried morels, place them in a bowl and cover with lukewarm water. Stir to wash the grit off. Carefully lift the morels from the water and transfer them to a clean bowl. Cover with cold water and leave to soak for 15 minutes.

Place the baby carrots in a saucepan with a little water and cook until just tender.

Heat the butter in a non-stick frying pan and brown the chicken fillets for 2 minutes on each side. Season with salt and pepper. Transfer to a small ovenproof dish and bake for 15 minutes.

Add the shallots to the frying pan and stir for 1 minute. Drain the morels, reserving the soaking liquid. Add them to the pan, season with salt and pepper and sweat for 5 minutes over a medium heat. Add the soaking liquid and bring to a simmer. Add the veal stock and cream and simmer until the liquid has reduced by half.

Add the chicken and carrots to the morel sauce. Baste the chicken with the sauce for 30 seconds. Add the chopped parsley and lemon juice, stir and serve.

Serves 2

CHICKEN FRICASSÉE WITH ARTICHOKES

Poulet aux artichauts
From the Provence Region

The sun shines abundantly at the border of the northern part of Provence, and the local artichokes and tomatoes make a superb, delicate accompaniment to the region's many fine chicken dishes.

3 small artichokes
1 slice lemon
1 tablespoon extra-virgin olive oil
2 chicken drumsticks
   on the bone, skin on
2 chicken thighs on the bone,
   skin on
salt
freshly ground black pepper

1 teaspoon coriander seeds
½ teaspoon fennel seeds
½ small brown onion,
   finely chopped
1 teaspoon tomato paste
50 ml dry white wine
2 tomatoes, cut into small dice
2 tablespoons chopped parsley

Cut two-thirds off the top of the artichokes, using a serrated knife. Then use a paring knife to carefully trim away all the leaves so you are left with the artichoke heart. Trim the artichoke stalks leaving about 2 cm. Using a melon baller or spoon, remove the hairy part of the heart, then cut the heart into quarters. Rub the clean artichoke pieces with a slice of lemon to prevent discolouring, then place them in a bowl of cold water until required.

Heat the oil in a medium frying pan and brown the chicken pieces for 2 minutes on each side. Season the chicken with salt and pepper.

Drain the artichoke pieces, add them to the pan and stir over the heat for 2 minutes. Add the coriander and fennel seeds and stir briefly, then add the chopped onion and cook for 3 minutes. Stir in the tomato paste and white wine and bring to the boil. Stir in the chopped tomatoes and bring to a simmer. Cover with a lid and cook over a low heat for 15–20 minutes.

To serve, spoon a little sauce and some artichokes onto two plates. Top with the chicken pieces, sprinkle with chopped parsley and serve.

Serves 2

CHICKEN AND PRAWN CASSEROLE

Poulet aux gambas

From the Languedoc/Roussillon Region

It's very Mediterranean to cook chicken and prawns together, especially with spices such as chilli and saffron (like a paella). Gambas are large prawns – they are fleshy and succulent.

4 tablespoons extra-virgin
  olive oil

1 brown onion, chopped

4 chicken pieces on the bone
  (thighs are good)

salt

freshly ground pepper

1 mild green chilli, finely sliced

2 large tomatoes, peeled,
  seeded and chopped

3 tablespoons Vermouth

a pinch of saffron threads

8 raw king prawns, shells on

4 tablespoons roasted pine nuts,
  finely chopped

3 tablespoons chopped parsley

2 cloves garlic, chopped

Heat 1 tablespoon of the oil in a frying pan and cook the onion over a low heat for 5 minutes.

Season the chicken pieces with salt and pepper. Heat another 2 tablespoons of oil in a wide saucepan and brown the chicken pieces all over. Add the onion to the pan, together with the chilli, tomato, Vermouth and saffron. Bring to a simmer, cover with a lid and cook for 20 minutes. Turn the chicken pieces over once during the cooking.

Heat the remaining oil in a large frying pan and cook the prawns for 1 minute on each side Add the prawns to the pan with the chicken, stir gently and cook for 2 minutes more. Stir in the chopped pine nuts, parsley and garlic and serve immediately.

Serves about 4

POACHED CHICKEN WITH VEGETABLES

Poule au pot

From the Béarn/Pyrenees Region by Elizabeth Kerdelhué

The French, me included, adore their poule au pot. In the depths of winter it is really lovely comfort food. Poule au pot is easy to prepare and is very healthy. The tasty cooking broth is served separately as a soup, to which small pasta is sometimes added.

1 x 1.8 kg free-range chicken,
    skin on or off, according to taste
a few sprigs thyme
a few sprigs parsley
1 bay leaf
1 medium brown onion, peeled
3 cloves
8 black peppercorns
salt
freshly ground black pepper
4 medium carrots, peeled

4 medium turnips, peeled
2 leeks, washed and cut into
    10 cm lengths
2 sticks celery, cut into
    10 cm lengths
2 teaspoons mustard
2 tablespoons red wine vinegar
6 tablespoons olive oil
6 gherkins, thinly sliced
2 tablespoons chopped parsley

Put the chicken in a large pot, cover with water and place it on a medium heat.

Use kitchen string to tie the thyme, parsley and bay leaf together to make a bouquet garni. Stud the onion with the cloves and add to the pot with bouquet garni and peppercorns and season with salt and pepper.

Add the vegetables to the pot, bring to a simmer and cook for about 50 minutes. Remove surface foam from time to time with a large spoon or skimmer.

In a small bowl, mix the mustard with a little salt and pepper. Whisk in the vinegar, then add the oil, whisking continuously. Stir in gherkins and parsley.

Transfer the chicken and vegetables to a platter and serve with the dressing either poured over the top or in a separate jug. Serve the broth separately, with or without pasta.

Serves 4

CHICKEN BURGUNDY

Coq au vin
From the Burgundy Region

This is one of the first classic French dishes I learned to prepare as an eighteen-year-old chef in Paris. There are several versions of the dish and if you have time you can marinate the chicken in the wine overnight.

20 small onions (pickling onions), peeled
50 g butter
100 g bacon, cut into thin strips
250 g mushrooms
8 chicken pieces on the bone (e.g. 4 drumsticks and 4 thighs)
sea salt
freshly ground black pepper
30 ml Cognac

1 large tablespoon plain flour
400 ml good red wine
1 sprig thyme
a few sprigs parsley
1 bay leaf
1 clove garlic
2 tablespoons tomato paste
2 tablespoons chopped parsley

Place the onions in a saucepan with plenty of cold water and bring to the boil. Boil for 2 minutes then drain well.

Melt half the butter in a large ovenproof saucepan or casserole dish. Add the onions and brown them over a medium heat for a few minutes. Add the bacon and stir well for 2 minutes. Add the mushrooms and cook for 4–5 minutes until the mushrooms are soft. Transfer the onions, bacon and mushrooms to a dish.

Add the remaining butter to the pan and brown the chicken pieces over a high heat for a few minutes. Season with salt and pepper and stir well.

Drain off excess fat into a bowl and discard.

Add the Cognac to the pan and carefully flame the chicken pieces. (It is safest to do this away from the stove). Stir well, then sprinkle on the flour. Pour in the wine and shake the pan.

Use kitchen string to tie the thyme, parsley and bay leaf together to make a bouquet garni.

Add to the pan, together with the garlic and tomato paste, and stir well. Bring to a slow simmer, cover with a lid and cook for about 20 minutes.

Turn the chicken pieces over and add the mushrooms, bacon and onions to the pan and simmer for a further 10 minutes. Check the seasoning, sprinkle with chopped parsley and serve.

Serves 4

Note: If you prefer a thicker sauce, pour it into a separate saucepan and boil until reduced to your liking.

CHICKEN CASSEROLE COOKED IN RIESLING

Poulet au riesling

From the Alsace Region

The white wines of Alsace made with riesling grapes are outstanding and in true French tradition, a region with great wine also offers wonderful gastronomy. This dish is a fine example of a festive Alsatian dish.

12 parsley stalks
1 bay leaf
2 sprigs thyme
4 chicken drumsticks
  (skin on or off)
4 chicken thighs
  (skin on or off)
salt
freshly ground black pepper
1 tablespoon oil

20 g butter
2 shallots, chopped
30 ml Cognac (or brandy)
200 ml Alsace riesling
a little grated nutmeg (optional)
300 g baby mushrooms
juice of ½ lemon
100 ml cream
2 egg yolks
3 tablespoons chopped parsley

Use kitchen string to tie the thyme, parsley and bay leaf together to make a bouquet garni. Season the chicken pieces with salt and pepper. Heat the oil and half the butter in a large heavy-based saucepan. Brown the chicken pieces over a high heat for 2–3 minutes. Add the shallots, shake the pan and cook for 2 minutes.

Add the Cognac to the pan, stir well, then carefully flame the chicken pieces. (It is safest to do this away from the stove). When the flame dies down, pour in the wine and add the nutmeg and bouquet garni. Bring to a slow simmer, cover with a lid and cook for about 25 minutes.

Meanwhile, melt the remaining butter in a frying pan. Sauté the mushrooms until just tender. Add them to the chicken and simmer for 3 minutes. Stir in the lemon juice.

In a medium bowl, whisk together the cream and egg yolks. Pour in 1 cup of the hot cooking liquid from the chicken, whisking continuously. Pour the mixture back into the pan and stir gently over a low heat for a few minutes (it must not boil). Remove the bouquet garni, add the chopped parsley, and serve.

Serves 4

GRILLED DUCK WITH SAUTÉED POTATOES AND CURLY SALAD

Canard grillé, pommes de terre sautées, salade frisée

From the Languedoc Region by Philippe Mouchel

This duck recipe is very simple to prepare and a lovely example of a rustic French dish that can be served when a few good friends come to dinner.

3 duck legs

1 tablespoon sea salt

freshly ground black pepper

3 teaspoons finely grated lemon zest

2 tablespoons goose fat (available from specialist butchers and good delicatessens)

2 large potatoes, peeled and cut into 1cm cubes

2 cloves garlic, 1 crushed and 1 finely chopped

1 red onion, cut into long thin pieces

salt

freshly ground black pepper

1 cup mushrooms, quartered

1 tablespoon chopped thyme

1 tablespoon rosemary leaves

1 tablespoon butter

1 teaspoon Dijon mustard

1 tablespoon cherry vinegar or other vinegar

3 tablespoons olive oil

3 cups curly endive, roughly torn

3 sprigs thyme to garnish

Preheat the oven grill to high.

Rub the duck legs all over with sea salt, paying special attention to the skin side.

Place the duck legs on a rack set in a roasting tray. Season the duck skin with pepper and lemon zest. Place under the hot grill and cook until the skins have browned a little. Turn off the grill element and set the oven temperature to 200°C. Cook the duck legs for about 30 minutes.

Meanwhile, heat the goose fat in a large frying pan. Add the potatoes and stir over a medium heat for 2–3 minutes. Add the crushed garlic clove and onion and stir for 2 minutes. Season with salt and pepper. Add the mushrooms and cook for about 8 minutes, or until the potatoes and mushrooms are tender. Add the thyme, rosemary and a knob of butter.

In a large salad bowl mix the chopped garlic clove with the mustard, cherry vinegar and a little salt and pepper. Whisk in the oil. Add the curly endive to the bowl and toss well in the dressing.

Divide the potatoes between three plates. Top with a duck leg, garnish with a sprig of thyme and serve with the endive salad.

Serves 3

une baguette

ⓐ pas trop cuite
ⓑ plutôt bien cuite
ⓒ coupée en deux

ROAST DUCK FILLET WITH CHERRIES

Canard aux cerises
From the Pyrenees Region

The scenery in the Pyrenees mountain ranges is stunning. Fruit groves thrive in the valleys between the peaks, and during the hot summers the local sweet cherries make a superb accompaniment to duck, one of the most popular festive dishes of the region.

2–3 medium potatoes,
   peeled and quartered
80 ml milk
20 g butter
2 duck breast fillets, skin on
salt
freshly ground black pepper
1 tablespoon olive oil
2 tablespoons Portuguese port
   (or red wine)

2 tablespoons fresh orange juice
2 tablespoons veal glaze
   (available from good butchers
   and delicatessens)
12–20 cherries, stoned just
   before using
2 tablespoons chopped parsley

Preheat the oven to 150°C.

Boil the potatoes in lightly salted water until tender, then drain well.

Bring the milk and butter to the boil in a medium saucepan. Push the drained potatoes through a mouli into the hot milk. Stir well, then mix in 2 tablespoons of the butter. Set the potato purée aside and keep warm.

Meanwhile, use a sharp knife to score the skin of the duck fillets in a criss-cross pattern. Season with salt and pepper.

Heat the olive oil in small roasting tray and brown the duck fillets, skin-side down, for about 3 minutes. Turn the fillets over, then transfer to the oven for about 10 minutes.

When the duck fillets are cooked, transfer them to a warm plate and cover with foil.

Discard the excess fat from the pan, then add the port and bring to the boil. Add the orange juice and bring to a simmer. Add the veal glaze, return to a simmer, then add the pitted cherries and heat them through.

Just before serving, gently reheat the potato. Divide the potato between two deep plates and arrange a duck fillet on top. Garnish with cherries, spoon on the sauce, sprinkle with chopped parsley and serve.

Serves 2

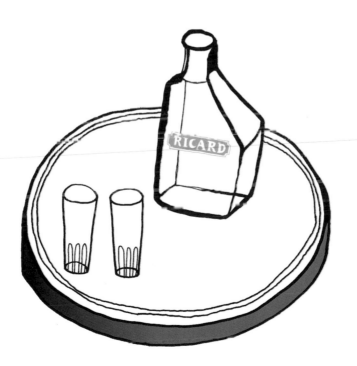

DUCK CASSEROLE IN RED WINE

Daube de canard

From the Gascogne/Pyrenees Region by Philippe Mouchel

A casserole of duck legs cooked slowly in red wine and flavoured with aromatic herbs, orange zest and vegetables is called a 'daube'. It is one of my favourite dishes to enjoy with a good red wine on a cold winter's evening.

3 duck legs
250 ml good red wine
1 onion, diced
1 carrot, diced
2 cloves garlic, crushed
2 sprigs thyme
1 bay leaf

a few pieces orange zest
salt
freshly ground pepper
a little olive oil
500 g baby carrots
2 tablespoons chopped parsley

Place the duck legs in a bowl with the wine, onion, carrot, garlic, thyme, bay leaf and orange zest. Cover with plastic wrap and marinate overnight in the refrigerator.

Preheat the oven to 160°C.

Remove the duck legs from the marinade and pat them dry on a paper towel. Season with salt and pepper. Heat a little oil in a cast-iron saucepan or casserole dish and brown the duck legs on all sides. Use a slotted spoon to remove the vegetables and herbs from the marinade. Add them to the pan and stir for a few minutes. Pour in the marinade, stir and bring to a low simmer. Cover the pan with a lid and bake in the oven for about 1½ hours.

Meanwhile, peel the baby carrots and steam for a couple of minutes.

When the duck legs are almost cooked, remove them from the pan and strain the sauce, discarding the herbs and vegetables. Return the duck legs to the pan and add back the sauce. Add the baby carrots, cover the pan and return to the oven for 15 minutes.

Serve each duck leg topped with baby carrots. Spoon the glorious sauce over the top and serve sprinkled with chopped parsley.

Serves 3

CASSOULET

From the Gascogne Region by Philippe Mouchel

Cassoulet is a hearty dish of confit duck, baked beans, and various pork cuts, including sausages. It is one of the most popular French winter classics and features on restaurant menus in most family restaurants between Montpellier and Bordeaux. Confit duck and duck fat are both available from specialist butchers and good delicatessens.

1 tablespoon duck fat
  (or butter or olive oil)
¼ cup diced celery
¼ cup diced carrots
¼ cup diced onions
1 clove garlic, left whole
1 cup coco or haricot beans,
  soaked overnight in cold water
50 ml dry white wine
1 teaspoon tomato paste
1 bay leaf

2 sprigs thyme
salt
freshly ground black pepper
1 tablespoon olive oil
1–2 Toulouse sausages, or good
  quality pork sausages
200 g cooked pork knuckle
200 g cooked pork belly
2 confit duck legs
½ cup dried breadcrumbs
3 tablespoons chopped parsley

Preheat the oven to 150°C.

Heat the duck fat in an ovenproof dish over a medium heat. Add the celery, carrot, onion and garlic and sauté for a few minutes. Drain the soaked beans and add them to the dish. Add the wine, stir well and bring to the boil. Add enough water to cover and bring to a simmer. Add the tomato paste, bay leaf and thyme and season with a little salt and pepper. Cover with a lid and cook for 1–1 ½ hours, or until the beans are almost cooked.

Heat the oil in a frying pan and brown the sausages all over. Add them to the ovenproof dish, along with the pork knuckle, pork belly and duck legs. Shake the dish to distribute the beans evenly, then sprinkle on the breadcrumbs.

Return the dish to the oven and cook, uncovered, for 30 minutes until the breadcrumbs are crisp and brown.

Sprinkle with chopped parsley and serve. French people love to eat cassoulet with mustard but my wife doesn't!

Serves 2–3

RABBIT STEW WITH PRUNES

Lapin aux pruneaux

From the Béarn/Pyrenees Region by Philippe Mouchel

Rabbit was an extremely popular meat during my youth in rural France. My family kept rabbits in the backyard, and we fed them with vegetable scraps and used the manure to fertilise our vegetable garden.

1 x 1.5 kg rabbit, cut into
  6–8 pieces
18 prunes, stones removed
½ bottle good red wine
1 tablespoon honey
1 cinnamon stick
1 star anise
salt
freshly ground black pepper

1 tablespoon olive oil
20 g butter
1 small brown onion, diced
1 small carrot, diced
3 sprigs thyme
1 slice pain d'épice
  (spiced honey bread)
3 tablespoons chopped parsley

Preheat the oven to 150°C.

Place the prunes in a bowl. Combine the wine, honey, cinnamon stick and star anise in a saucepan. Bring to the boil then pour over the prunes.

Season the rabbit pieces with salt and pepper. Heat the oil and half the butter in an oven-proof saucepan or casserole dish and brown the rabbit pieces all over. Tip any excess fat out of the pan and add the remaining butter. Stir in the diced onion and carrot, cover with a lid and cook for a few minutes.

Add the soaked prunes, together with their soaking liquor and spices. Finally, add the thyme and pain d'épice, which will soften and thicken the sauce as it cooks. Cover the pan and cook for about 2 hours, stirring a couple of times during the cooking. When cooked, the rabbit meat should fall away from the bones.

Sprinkle with chopped parsley and serve.

Serves 6

RABBIT CASSEROLE WITH CAPSICUM AND OLIVES

Lapin aux poivrons et aux olives

From the Northwest Provence Region by Philippe Mouchel

Wild Provençal herbs and wild rabbits are both plentiful around the incredible Mont Ventoux, one of the greatest mountain challenges for the riders of the Tour de France.

1 red capsicum
6 very small pickling onions, peeled
6 rabbit pieces, on the bone
salt
freshly ground black pepper
4 tablespoons extra-virgin olive oil

4 cloves garlic, peeled
2 rashers bacon, finely sliced
20 black olives
1 small red chilli, roughly chopped
1 sprig rosemary, roughly chopped
100 ml dry white wine
250 ml strong chicken stock or rabbit stock

Preheat the oven to 200°C. Wrap the capsicum in foil and bake in the oven for about 20 minutes. Remove from the oven, carefully open the foil and peel the capsicum. Cut it in half, remove the seeds and cut each half into 3 pieces.

Reduce the oven temperature to 160°C.

Place the onions in a saucepan with plenty of cold water and bring to the boil. Boil for 2 minutes then drain well.

Season the rabbit pieces with salt and pepper. Heat 2 tablespoons of the olive oil in a cast-iron saucepan or casserole and brown the rabbit pieces for a few minutes. Add the capsicum, baby onions, garlic, bacon, olives, chilli and rosemary. Stir well, cover with a lid and cook over a low heat for 10 minutes.

Add the white wine to the pan, bring to the boil and cook until reduced to about 2 tablespoons. Add the stock, bring to a simmer, cover with a lid and bake in the oven for about 1 ½ hours, or until the rabbit is cooked.

Lift the rabbit pieces onto a serving plate. Add the remaining 2 tablespoons of olive oil to the pot with the sauce and vegetables. Bring to the boil and cook for a few minutes to thicken it.

Spoon the vegetables and sauce over the rabbit and serve.

Serves 2

RABBIT WITH A DIJON MUSTARD SAUCE

Lapin à la moutarde de Dijon
From the Burgundy Region

Dijon, the capital of Burgundy, is a great city to visit, not only for its splendid architecture, but because of its world-famous mustard.

6 rabbit hind legs	2 cloves garlic, crushed
a little sea salt	1 brown onion, chopped
freshly ground black pepper	150 ml dry white wine
a little plain flour for dusting	2 cups mushrooms, halved or
2 tablespoons olive oil	quartered, depending on size
20 g butter	2 tablespoons Dijon mustard
a few sprigs thyme, chopped	2 tablespoons cream
150 g bacon, cut into small pieces	1 egg yolk
1 bay leaf	2 tablespoons chopped parsley

Preheat the oven to 150°C.

Season the rabbit legs with a little salt and pepper and dust with a little flour.

Heat the oil and butter in an ovenproof casserole over a medium heat and brown the rabbit legs all over. Add the thyme, bacon, bay leaf, garlic and onion and stir well for 3–5 minutes. Stir in the wine, then add the mushrooms and stir again. Cover with a lid and cook for about 1–1 ½ hours. (If using wild rabbit, it may take a little longer.)

Transfer the casserole to the stove top over a low heat.

In a bowl, whisk together the mustard cream and egg yolk. Slowly stir this mixture into the hot casserole, taking care not to let the sauce boil. Keep over a low heat for 5 minutes for the mustard flavour to infuse the rabbit.

Divide the rabbit pieces between six plates, spoon on the sauce and sprinkle with chopped parsley. Serve with your choice of vegetables.

Serves 6

WILD RABBIT WITH MUSHROOMS

Lapin de Garenne aux champignons

From the South of the Loire/Centre Region by Philippe Mouchel

Wild rabbit abounds in the forested rural regions south of the Loire. In autumn and winter, rabbits feature on the table of many farm houses and the favourite accompaniment is wild mushrooms. I prepare this dish using field mushrooms mixed with a few Swiss browns and shiitake mushrooms.

1 wild rabbit (about 1 kg),
   cut into 8 pieces
salt
freshly ground pepper
2 tablespoons olive oil
60 g butter
3 cloves garlic, peeled and crushed
3 shallots, diced
1 stick celery, diced

400 g mixed mushrooms of
   your choice, quartered
150 ml dry white wine
250 ml strong veal stock
   or rabbit stock
1 sprig thyme
10 green peppercorns
1 tablespoon tarragon leaves

Preheat the oven to 150°C.

Season the rabbit pieces with salt and pepper. Heat the olive oil in a cast-iron saucepan or casserole dish and brown the rabbit pieces on all sides. Add about a third of the butter to the pan, followed by the garlic, shallots, celery and about 10 of the quartered mushrooms. Stir well, cover with a lid and cook over a low heat for about 5 minutes.

Add the wine to the pan, bring to the boil and boil for 2 minutes. Add the stock, thyme and green peppercorns, cover with a lid and bake for about 2 hours, or until the rabbit is tender, stirring once or twice during the cooking.

Fifteen minutes before you are ready to serve, heat another third of the butter in a frying pan. Add the remaining mushrooms and sauté until just tender. Set aside and keep warm.

Transfer the rabbit pieces to a dish, and cover with foil to keep warm.

Reduce the sauce by half, then stir in the remaining butter. Spoon the sauce and mushrooms over the rabbit pieces, garnish with tarragon leaves and serve.

Serves 3

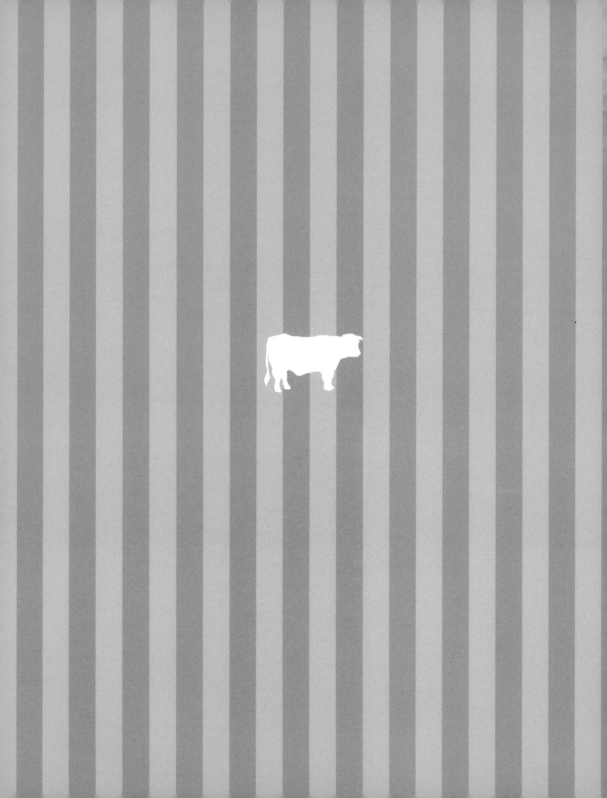

CHAPTER FOUR

BEEF, LAMB & PORK

EYE FILLET STEAK WITH BÉARNAISE SAUCE

Tournedos sauce béarnaise

From the Pyrenees/Béarn Region by Philippe Mouchel

The delicious béarnaise sauce that is served with this steak was named after the region of Béarn in the north-west of the Pyrenees. If you prefer, cook the steaks on a barbecue.

4 x 150 g eye fillet steaks
  (or another steak of your choice)
salt
freshly ground pepper
1 tablespoon olive oil
1 teaspoon butter
Béarnaise Sauce
2 medium shallots, finely chopped

30 ml white wine vinegar
2 tablespoons tarragon leaves
30 ml white wine
4 black peppercorns, crushed
120 g butter, cut into small cubes
2 egg yolks
salt
freshly ground pepper

To make the béarnaise sauce, combine the shallots, vinegar, half the tarragon, the white wine and crushed peppercorns in a saucepan. Bring to a simmer and cook until the liquid has reduced to about 1 tablespoon.

Meanwhile, melt the butter in a small saucepan over a low heat without allowing it to boil.

Place the egg yolks in a medium metal or glass bowl and whisk in the shallot reduction. Sit the bowl over a saucepan of hot water, taking care that the bowl doesn't touch the water. Keep the pan over a low heat as the water must be hot but not boiling. Continue whisking the yolks briskly until they become thick and foamy. After about 5 minutes they should have doubled in volume.

Remove from the saucepan and very slowly pour in the melted butter, whisking continuously until well incorporated. The finished sauce should be creamy but not too runny. Add the rest of the tarragon and season with salt and pepper.

Season the steaks with salt and pepper.

Heat the oil in a frying pan and cook the steaks over a high heat for 3–5 minutes on each side, depending on how you like them cooked. Towards the end of the cooking, add the butter to the pan and baste the steaks. Season with salt and pepper and serve on hot plates. Serve the sauce separately.

Serves 4

ROAST BEEF FILLET WITH FRENCH-STYLE PEAS

Rôti de boeuf et petits pois à la Française
From the Limousin Region by Philippe Mouchel

The Limousin region in the heart of France is famous for its superb Limousin cattle breed. The garnish of peas cooked with lettuce is a classic and much loved by the French.

1 x 600 g beef eye fillet,
   tied with kitchen string
salt
cracked black pepper
1 tablespoon olive oil
2 tablespoons butter
1 shallot, chopped
100 ml red wine
2 tablespoons veal glaze,
   (available from good
   butchers and delicatessens)
3 tablespoons water
1 sprig thyme

French-style Peas
1 tablespoon olive oil
2 ½ tablespoons butter
1 brown onion, sliced
1 cos lettuce heart, washed and cut
   into bite-size pieces, plus a few extra
   small cos lettuce leaves for garnish
   (optional)
3 slices prosciutto ham, cut into pieces
1 clove garlic, finely chopped
500 g shelled peas
1 sprigs thyme
250 ml chicken stock

Preheat the oven to 180°C.

Season the beef with salt and cracked pepper. Heat the oil and 1 tablespoon of the butter in a roasting tray, then brown the meat on all sides, basting well. Transfer to the oven for 15–20 minutes, or until cooked to your liking. Remove the string, wrap the meat in foil and leave to rest for 10 minutes.

Tip the cooking fat out of the roasting tray then add another tablespoon of butter. Add the shallots and stir over a medium heat for 2 minutes. Add the red wine and boil until reduced to about 2 tablespoons. Add the veal glaze and water and bring to the boil. Season with a little cracked pepper and add the thyme. Tip the sauce into a smaller saucepan and keep hot.

To prepare the French-style peas, heat the oil and 2 tablespoons of the butter in a saucepan. Add the onion and cook for 5 minutes. Add the lettuce, prosciutto, garlic, peas, thyme and chicken stock and simmer for 10 minutes.

When ready to serve, reheat the beef in a frying pan with the remaining butter for 1–2 minutes. Carve into 8 slices. Divide the peas between four plates and top with slices of beef. If you wish, add a little extra butter to the hot sauce, then spoon it over the beef. Garnish with lettuce leaves, if using, and serve straight away.

Serves 4

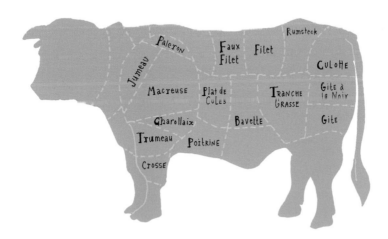

BEEF FILLET WITH TRUFFLES AND FOIE GRAS

Filet de boeuf aux truffes et foie gras
From the Périgord Region

Every year French gourmets look forward to the truffle season, which starts with the first frost and finishes with the last, (i.e. from November to February). If you are able to source a fresh truffle then do try this classic dish.

2 medium potatoes,
  peeled and quartered
60 ml milk
3 tablespoons butter
2 x 200 g eye fillet steaks
2 teaspoons cracked
  black pepper

salt
2 teaspoons olive oil
1 small shallot, finely chopped
2 tablespoons Madeira
60 ml strong veal stock
10 g black truffle, thinly sliced
2 slices foie gras, each about 20 g

Boil the potatoes in lightly salted water until tender, then drain well.

Bring the milk to the boil in a medium saucepan. Push the drained potatoes through a mouli onto the hot milk. Stir well, then mix in 2 tablespoons of the butter. Set the potato purée aside and keep warm.

Season the steaks with cracked pepper and salt.

Heat the oil and ⅓ tablespoon of the remaining butter in a small frying pan. Fry the steaks over a high heat for 3–5 minutes on each side, depending on how you like them cooked. Transfer the steaks to a warm plate and cover with foil.

Add another ⅓ tablespoon of butter to the pan. Add the shallot and stir for 2 minutes over a medium heat. Add the Madeira and bring to the boil. Add the stock, return to the boil and boil for 1 minute. Add the rest of the butter and season to taste. Stir in the sliced truffles.

Just before serving, gently reheat the potato. Divide the potato between two plates and place a steak on top. Arrange a slice of foie gras on top of each steak, spoon on a little sauce and serve.

Serves 2

BEEF RIB EYE WITH RED WINE SAUCE AND VEGETABLE PURÉE

Côte de boeuf sauce au vin rouge purée de légumes

From the Limousin Region (Centre)

If you're looking for a great dish to serve with a special bottle of red wine, this is it. It's easy to prepare but take care not to overcook the beef, and make sure you rest it for at least 5 minutes before carving.

½ tablespoon olive oil

1 x 400–500 g beef rib eye

250 g fresh peas

2 small carrots,
cut into small pieces

30 g butter

salt

freshly ground pepper

1 shallot, finely chopped

2 tablespoons red wine

60 ml strong beef stock

Preheat the oven to 200°C.

Heat the oil in a roasting tray and brown each side of the rib eye for about 2 minutes. Then transfer to the oven and cook for 10–15 minutes, depending on how you like it cooked.

Cook the peas and carrots in boiling water in separate saucepans. Drain each well, then blend them separately with a little of the butter. Season with salt and pepper and keep them warm in the saucepans.

When the rib eye is cooked, transfer it to a warm plate, cover with foil and leave to rest for about 5 minutes.

Melt the remaining butter in the roasting tray. Add the shallot and cook over a low heat for 2 minutes. Add the red wine and bring to the boil. Add the beef stock and simmer for 2–3 minutes.

Carve the beef into 1 cm slices. Spoon the pea and carrot purées onto 2 plates. Top with a few slices of beef, spoon on the red wine sauce and serve.

Serves 2

RIB OF BEEF WITH RED WINE SAUCE

Côte de boeuf à la Bordelaise

From the Bordeaux/Southwest Region by Philippe Mouchel

It's a matter of taste, but for many people there are no better red wines in the world than the fine wines of Bordeaux in the southwest of France. This dish of beef ribs with red wine sauce is a perfect match for the Bordeaux wines. This beef is lovely served with sautéed mushrooms.

2 tablespoons vegetable oil
2 x 400 g beef ribs,
   each about 5 cm thick
sea salt
freshly cracked black pepper
3 tablespoons butter
2 shallots, chopped

100 ml Bordeaux
   red wine (or another red)
125 ml rich veal or
   beef stock
a few sprigs parsley
80 g bone marrow

Heat the oil in a heavy frying pan and cook the beef ribs on one side for 4–5 minutes. Season the meat with salt and pepper, turn and cook for another 4–5 minutes, adding 1 tablespoon of butter to the pan and basting the meat from time to time. Transfer the cooked beef ribs to a dish, cover with foil and leave to rest in a warm place.

Tip out any excess fat from the frying pan then add another tablespoon of butter. Add the shallots and stir over a medium heat for a few minutes. Add the wine and boil for a few minutes until reduced by at least half. Add the stock and simmer for 5 minutes. Whisk in the final tablespoon of butter and add the parsley.

Meanwhile, place the bone marrow in a small saucepan of cold salted water and bring to a simmer. Poach over a low heat for 5 minutes, then drain well.

Cut each rib into slices, arrange on plates and serve with thin slices of the bone marrow. Spoon on the red wine sauce and serve.

Serves 3

BEEF BURGUNDY

Boeuf Bourguignon
From the Burgundy Region

This is one of the most famous French regional dishes. Allow enough time to cook the dish slowly and well. It's perfect for a winter dinner party as it can be prepared in advance and enjoyed with a great red wine.

800 g beef cheek (or another casserole cut such as oyster blade)

1 brown onion, finely sliced

2 shallots, finely sliced

2 cloves garlic, crushed

1 sprig thyme or a 6 cm sprig rosemary

300 ml red wine

3 tablespoons olive oil

salt

freshly ground black pepper

2 teaspoons butter

1 tablespoon plain flour

120 g bacon, cut into small pieces

16 baby onions

25 small mushrooms

4 tablespoons chopped parsley

The day before you cook the dish, trim the beef of excess fat and sinews and cut it into 4–6 pieces. Place in a bowl with the onion, shallot, crushed garlic and the thyme or rosemary. Cover with wine and stir in 1 tablespoon of the olive oil.

The following day lift the meat, onion, garlic and shallots from the wine and place on a towel to dry. Reserve the wine and herbs as well. Season the meat with salt and pepper.

Preheat the oven to 140°C.

Heat 1 tablespoon of oil in an ovenproof saucepan or casserole dish and brown the meat on all sides. Add the butter to the pan, followed by the reserved onions, shallots and garlic, and stir well. Sprinkle on the flour and stir well. Add the reserved wine and stir well, then add the herbs. Cover with a lid and cook for about 2 hours, or until the meat is tender.

Meanwhile, heat the remaining tablespoon of olive oil in a frying pan and sauté the bacon over a medium heat for a few minutes. Remove the bacon and set aside. Add the baby onions and brown well all over. Set aside the onions and cook the mushrooms for 2 minutes.

Towards the end of the 2 hours, add the bacon, onions and mushrooms to the casserole and stir in well. Return to the oven and cook for a further 20 minutes.

Serve sprinkled with chopped parsley.

Serves 4

BEEF AND BEER STEW

Carbonnade de boeuf

From the Northern Region by Philippe Mouchel

In the north of France beer is much more popular than wine. It is often used in cooking, as in this flavoursome winter beef casserole. It is traditional to serve this stew with large croutons spread with mustard.

50 ml vegetable oil
50 g butter
4 beef cheeks or 1 kg oyster
  blade steak, trimmed of
  excess fat and sinews
3 large onions, thinly sliced
2 teaspoons brown sugar
2 tablespoons red wine vinegar
40 g plain flour
750 ml beer (dark beer is
  often used in France)

250 ml beef stock
salt
freshly ground black pepper
a pinch of nutmeg
2 sprigs thyme
a few sprigs parsley
1 bay leaf
3 tablespoons chopped parsley
12 baby carrots

Preheat the oven to 140°C.

Heat half the oil and half the butter in a cast-iron saucepan or casserole dish and brown the beef on all sides. Transfer the beef to a plate.

Add the remaining oil and butter to the pan and cook the onions over a medium heat for about 10 minutes, or until they are soft and lightly browned. Sprinkle in the brown sugar and add the vinegar. Stir in the flour and cook for a few minutes. Add the beer, stock, salt, pepper and nutmeg.

Use kitchen string to tie the thyme, parsley and bay leaf together to make a bouquet garni. Add to the pan with the meat and bring to a simmer. Skim the surface then transfer to the oven for 3 hours, or until the meat is very tender.

Remove the casserole from the oven and add the baby carrots. Cook on top of the stove for 10–12 minutes, or until the carrots are tender. Sprinkle with chopped parsley and serve.

Serves 4

GRILLED LOIN OF LAMB WITH RATATOUILLE AND TAPENADE

Agneau grillé avec ratatouille et tapenade
From the Provence Region

This superb lamb dish is a perfect example of the flavoursome cuisine of Provence.
The ratatouille is also wonderful served on its own.

4 loins of lamb,
    each about 12 cm long
2 tablespoons olive oil,
    plus extra for drizzling
freshly ground black pepper
1 clove garlic, finely chopped
2 tablespoons rosemary leaves,
    finely chopped
salt

Ratatouille
3 tablespoons olive oil
½ brown onion, finely diced

2 sprigs thyme, chopped
1 clove garlic, finely chopped
1 small red capsicum, diced
1 small zucchini, diced
1 small eggplant, diced
3 tomatoes, diced

Tapenade
100 g pitted black olives
3 anchovies
1 tablespoon capers
2 tablespoons olive oil

To make the ratatouille, heat the oil in a saucepan over a medium heat. Add the onion and thyme and fry for a few minutes. Stir in the garlic, then add the capsicum and stir for a few minutes. Add the zucchini, eggplant and tomatoes, bring to a simmer and cook over a low heat for 20–30 minutes until the vegetables are soft. Refrigerate until required. It may be reheated as you need it.

To make the tapenade, blend all ingredients to a paste. Store in the refrigerator until 10 minutes before serving.

Season the lamb loins with olive oil, pepper, garlic and rosemary, then marinate in the refrigerator for at least 30 minutes.

Grill the lamb for 3–4 minutes on each side. Turn off the heat, cover the meat and leave it to rest for at least 5 minutes before slicing.

Serve the lamb loins on a bed of hot ratatouille. Season with salt and top each loin with a tablespoon of tapenade. Drizzle with the extra olive oil and serve.

Serves 4

ROAST LAMB WITH TARBAIS BEANS

Rôti d'agneau aux haricots Tarbais

From the Gascogne-Pyrenees Region by Philippe Mouchel

The cuisine north of the Pyrenees, around the city of Tarbes, is known as one of the most rustic in France and its tasty bean dishes are on offer on many restaurant menus as well as being very popular at home.

If you are unable to find Tarbais beans, then use other dried beans of your choice, such as borlotti or canellini. They need to be soaked for 24 hours in cold water.

Tarbais Beans

80 g dried beans of your choice
   (Tarbais, borlotti, canellini),
   soaked for 24 hours in cold water

1 small carrot, cut into pieces

1 stick of celery, cut into pieces

½ onion, left whole

1 clove garlic

4 sprigs thyme, plus extra to garnish

½ bay leaf

4–5 peppercorns

1 x 6–8 point lamb rack

salt

freshly ground black pepper

a little olive oil

2 cloves garlic

4 sprigs thyme

20 g butter

2 shallots, finely chopped

½ tablespoon chopped thyme

2 teaspoons red wine vinegar

2 tablespoons chopped parsley

To prepare the Tarbais beans, drain the soaked beans and place them in a saucepan with plenty of cold water. Add the carrot, celery, onion, 1 clove garlic, 1 sprig of thyme, ½ bay leaf and the peppercorns. Bring to a simmer and cook over a low heat for about 1 ½ hours, or until the beans are tender.

Preheat the oven to 180°C.

Season the lamb with salt and pepper. Heat a little oil in a roasting tray. Add the lamb rack and top with the garlic and thyme sprigs. Roast the lamb for about 5 minutes, then turn the rack over and roast the other side for 5 minutes. Remove from the oven and leave to rest for 5 minutes in a warm place.

Meanwhile, drain the beans and remove the vegetables and herbs. Heat the butter in a saucepan. Add the shallots and chopped thyme and stir for 1 minute.

Add the beans and heat through well. Stir in the red wine vinegar and parsley and season to taste.

When ready to serve, slice the lamb rack in half. Divide the beans between two plates and top with the lamb. Garnish with sprigs of thyme and drizzle a little olive oil over the top.

Serves 2

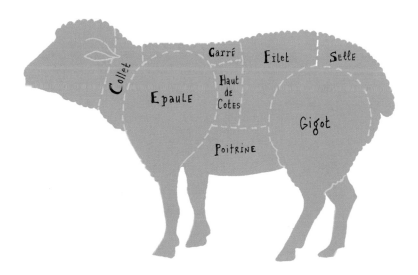

LAMB CASSEROLE WITH GREEN OLIVES

Ragoût de mouton aux olives vertes

From the Languedoc/Pyrenees Region by Philippe Mouchel

The Pyrenees region is famous for its tasty lamb, and this delicious casserole benefits from being cooked for a long time at a moderate temperature. When it's ready, the meat should be soft and tender.

800 g–1 kg deboned lamb
    shoulder, trimmed of excess
    fat and cut into large cubes
salt
freshly ground black pepper
2 tablespoons olive oil,
    plus extra for drizzling
1 teaspoon butter
½ medium carrot, diced
½ medium onion, diced
½ tablespoon tomato paste

150 ml dry white wine
3 cloves garlic, crushed
3 x 5 cm strips orange zest
15 green olives
300 ml chicken stock
1 large tomato, cut into 8
1 sprig thyme
1 bay leaf
a few basil leaves for garnishing

Preheat the oven to 140°C.

Season the lamb with salt and pepper. Heat the olive oil in an ovenproof saucepan or casserole dish and brown the lamb on all sides over a high heat.

Add the butter, followed by the carrot and onion and stir for 2 minutes. Add the tomato paste and stir well. Add the wine and bring to the boil. Add the garlic, orange peel, olives, chicken stock, tomato, thyme and bay leaf. Stir well and bring to a simmer. Cover with a lid and bake in the oven for about 3 hours, or until the meat is tender.

Garnish with basil leaves, drizzle with extra olive oil and serve.

Serves 4

SLOW-COOKED LEG OF LAMB

Gigot de sept heures

From the Pyrenees Region by Philippe Mouchel

This speciality of the Pyrenees region translates as 'seven-hour lamb'. You can cook it in a little less time if you do it at a higher temperature, but it won't be quite as succulent.

1 x 1.5 kg leg of lamb, trimmed
   of most visible fat
2 cloves garlic, peeled and cut
   into slivers
a little olive oil
2 sprigs thyme
a few sprigs parsley
1 bay leaf
sea salt

freshly ground black pepper
3 litres water or beef stock
3 carrots, cut into 2 cm slices
2 small turnips, quartered
2 leeks, washed and cut into
   2 cm pieces
1 onion, sliced
3 sticks celery, cut into 2 cm pieces
8 cloves garlic, chopped

Preheat the oven to 100–120°C.

Stud the trimmed leg of lamb with garlic slivers and tie with string. Heat the oil in a cast-iron casserole dish and brown the lamb all over.

Use kitchen string to tie the thyme, parsley and bay leaf together to make a bouquet garni. Add to the casserole dish and season the lamb with a little salt and pepper. Add the water or stock and bring to a simmer on top of the stove. Cover with a lid, then transfer to the oven for 5–6 hours. You can turn the lamb over in the casserole after 1 hour. During the cooking, the liquid may simmer very gently, but must not boil.

After 5–6 hours, tuck the carrots, turnips, leeks, onion, celery and garlic around the meat and cook for another hour.

Remove the casserole from the oven and carefully transfer the meat and vegetables onto a warm serving platter. Discard the bouquet garni and cover the platter with foil. On top of the stove reduce the remaining juices to about 500 ml.

When ready to serve, remove the string from the lamb. Pour sauce over the meat and vegetables and season with a little salt and pepper before carving at the table.

Serves 8

PAN-FRIED PORK CUTLETS WITH CABBAGE

Côtes de pork aux choux

From the Alsace Region by Philippe Mouchel

Alsatians love their food and take their cooking very seriously. Pork is the most popular meat at home and cabbage is the great speciality of this beautiful region.

10 cabbage leaves
2 free-range pork cutlets
salt
cracked pepper
3 tablespoons olive oil
2 ½ tablespoons butter
2 sprigs thyme
¼ onion, chopped

60 ml dry white wine
2 tablespoons veal glaze
   (available from good
   butchers and delicatessens)
1 tablespoon Dijon mustard
5 gherkins, cut into julienne strips
1 rasher bacon, diced

Preheat the oven to 170°C.

Cook the cabbage leaves in a large saucepan of boiling water for 3 minutes. Transfer them to a bowl of cold water and ice cubes, which helps them to cool quickly and keep their colour.

Season the pork cutlets with salt and pepper. Heat the oil and 1 tablespoon of butter in an ovenproof frying pan. Add the thyme and fry the pork cutlets for 1 minute on each side, then cook in the oven for about 5 minutes. Transfer the cutlets to a warm dish, cover with foil and leave to rest.

Heat another tablespoon of butter in the frying pan and cook the onion for 1 minute. Add the wine and boil until reduced to about 2 tablespoons. Stir in the veal glaze and bring to a simmer. Add the mustard and gherkins, stir well.

Meanwhile, cook the cabbage leaves again in boiling water for about 5 minutes, then drain.

Heat the remaining butter in a separate frying pan. Fry the bacon, stirring, for 2 minutes. Add the cabbage leaves and cook together for a few minutes.

Divide the cabbage between two plates. Arrange the pork cutlets on top, spoon on the sauce and serve.

Serves 2

ALSATIAN SAUERKRAUT

La choucroûte Alsacienne
From the Alsace Region by Philippe Mouchel

Alsatian sauerkraut is one of the best recognised French regional dishes. It's served in most Alsatian restaurants but also in many of the popular brasseries of Paris. It's often enjoyed with a glass of beer or Alsatian riesling. Sauerkraut, which literally means 'sour cabbage', is available at German-style delis and butchers, as are the pork cuts.

1 kg sauerkraut
20 g butter
1 large brown onion, sliced
2 bay leaves
3 cloves
12 juniper berries
600 g kassler (smoked and
    salted pork loin), cut
    into 6 slices

6 x 1 cm slices jagdwurst
    (or use strassburg or Polish sausage)
6 x 1 cm slices kaiserfleisch
    (smoked pork belly)
375 ml dry white wine,
    preferably Alsatian riesling
6 medium potatoes, peeled
6 thin Viennese sausages
3 tablespoons chopped parsley

Rinse the sauerkraut in cold water and squeeze out the excess moisture. This removes some of the sour flavour.

Melt the butter in a wide saucepan and gently fry the onion for 3 minutes. Sprinkle on half the sauerkraut and add the bay leaves, cloves and 6 juniper berries. Arrange the slices of kasseler, jagdwurst and kaiserfleisch on top then add the remaining sauerkraut and juniper berries. Pour on the wine, cover the pan tightly and simmer over a low heat for about 2 hours. This dish can also be cooked in a 150°C oven for 2 hours.

Half an hour before serving, boil the potatoes in lightly salted water until tender. Cook the Viennese sausages in simmering water for about 10 minutes.

Spoon the cabbage onto a large platter. Arrange the cooked meats and sausages on top and surround with the potatoes. Sprinkle with parsley and serve at the table with mustard or your favourite condiments.

Serves 6

BEAN STEW WITH TOULOUSE SAUSAGES

Cassoulet Toulousain

From the Languedoc/Gascogne Region by Stéphane Langlois

Every corner of the southwest of France has a different version of cassoulet. Around the town of Toulouse it's the local thick sausage that is the highlight of this popular French classic. Confit duck and duck fat are both available from specialist butchers and good delicatessens.

2 tablespoons duck fat
400 g salted pork, from the belly
   or shoulder, cut into 6 pieces
1 onion, diced
3 cloves garlic, crushed
1 carrot, sliced
2–3 sprigs of thyme,
   finely chopped
1 stick celery, diced
3 tablespoons plain flour
150 ml dry white wine

1 litre chicken stock
750 g cannellini beans,
   soaked overnight in cold water
3 tablespoons tomato paste
salt
freshly ground pepper
6 Toulouse sausages,
   or good quality pork sausages
6 confit duck legs
3 tablespoons chopped parsley

Melt the duck fat in a cast-iron saucepan or casserole dish. Add the pork pieces to the pan and brown for a few minutes. Add the onion and garlic and stir well. Add the carrot and thyme and stir again. Add the celery, then sprinkle on the flour and stir for 30 seconds. Stir in the wine, followed by the chicken stock. Add the cannellini beans and tomato paste, season with salt and pepper and bring to a simmer. Cover the pan and cook for about 1 hour over a low heat, or until the beans are almost cooked.

Add the sausages and simmer for a further 15 minutes. Add the duck legs and simmer gently for another 10 minutes.

To serve, spoon the beans and sauce into six deep soup plates. Top with a piece of pork, a duck leg and a sausage, sprinkle with chopped parsley and serve.

Serves 6

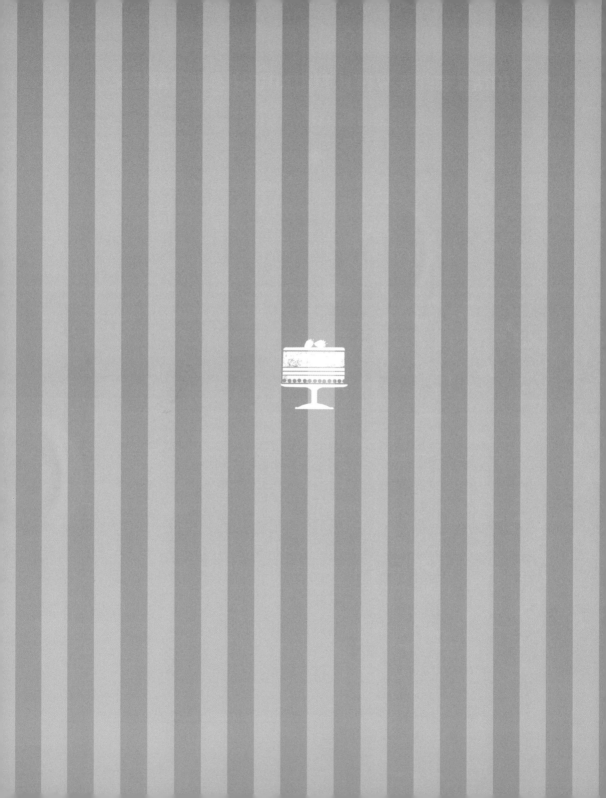

CHAPTER FIVE

❧

CAKES &
DESSERTS

APRICOT COMPOTE WITH ALMONDS AND ARMAGNAC WITH A EWE'S MILK YOGHURT

Compote d'abricots à l'Armagnac et aux amandes avec un yaourt de brebis
From the North Pyrenees Region

Using seasonal fruits, this simple French dessert is easy to prepare, and the ewe's milk yoghurt is a little more exotic. You can replace the Armagnac with another liqueur if you wish, or omit it altogether.

juice of 1 orange
juice of 1 lemon
½ cup caster sugar,
   plus 2 extra tablespoons
⅓ vanilla pod, split
   open lengthwise
12 ripe apricots,
   halved and stoned

2 tablespoons Armagnac
500 g ewe's milk yoghurt
100 ml cream
20 almonds, toasted
   and skinned

Combine the orange and lemon juice in a saucepan with the sugar and vanilla pod. Bring to a simmer. Add the apricots and return to a simmer. Cover the pan and cook the apricots over a low heat until soft. Transfer the apricots and syrup to a bowl, stir in the Armagnac and leave to cool. Refrigerate until 10 minutes before serving.

Whip the yoghurt with the cream and extra sugar until smooth.

When ready to serve, add the almonds to the apricots. Spoon a little yoghurt onto four serving plates. Top with the apricots and almonds and spoon on the syrup.

Serves 4

PEACHES POACHED IN SWEET WINE

Pêches poêlées au vin doux

From the Languedoc-Provence Region by Michael Gaté

These peaches poached in sweet wine make a superb finish to a summer dinner party.
Make sure the peaches are very sweet and just ripe when you buy them.

4 just ripe peaches, washed
30 g butter
4 tablespoons sugar
100 ml Muscat de Rivesaltes
   or another sweet white wine

200 g raspberries
2 tablespoons peeled,
   chopped pistachio nuts
icing sugar for dusting

Three-quarter fill a medium saucepan with water and bring to the boil. Gently drop in the peaches and simmer for 2 minutes. Drain the peaches and and place them in a bowl of cold water to cool. When cold, carefully peel the peaches. Cut them in half and remove the stones.

Melt the butter in a frying pan large enough to hold all the peaches. Add the sugar and stir briefly with a wooden spoon. When the sugar starts to brown, add the peach halves. Cook for 1–2 minutes then turn the peaches and shake the pan well. Add the muscat and bring to a simmer. Cover the pan with foil and cook for a few minutes until the peaches are cooked through.

To serve, place 2 peach halves on each plate. Garnish with raspberries and spoon on a little wine sauce. Sprinkle with pistachio nuts and dust with icing sugar. If you wish, serve with whipped cream or ice-cream.

Serves 2

POACHED PEACH AND CHERRY COUPE IN A LEMON SYRUP

Coupe de pêches et de cerises au citron
From the Languedoc Region

You can find this type of luscious, fruity dessert in the Languedoc region around the stunning city of Albi, the birth place of French painter, Toulouse Lautrec.

juice of 4 lemons	200 ml thickened cream
1 cup sugar	2 tablespoons full-cream milk
½ vanilla pod,	2 tablespoons sugar
split open lengthwise	sweet biscuits
6 peaches, washed and stoned	(waffles, cat's tongues,
500 g cherries, stoned	sponge fingers)

Combine the lemon juice, sugar and vanilla pod in a medium saucepan. Bring to a boil and cook for 30 seconds.

Cut each peach into 6–8 slices, but do not peel. Place in the simmering syrup and poach for 5–8 minutes. Use a slotted spoon to transfer the peach segments to a large bowl.

Return the syrup to a simmer and add the cherries. Stir gently then turn off the heat. The syrup must not boil. Pour the cherries and syrup over the peaches. Shake the bowl well then leave to cool. Once cold, refrigerate until 10 minutes before serving.

Whip the cream and milk together until light and firm, but not too stiff. Mix in the sugar.

Spoon the sweet cream into a piping bag fitted with a small serrated nozzle. Pipe a little cream into six serving glasses and top with a few peach segments and cherries. Top with a little more piped cream and finish with fruit. Serve straight away with your choice of sweet biscuits.

Serves 6

PEACH MELBA

Pêche Melba

From the Provence Region

Pêche Melba, one of the most well-known French desserts in the world, was created in 1892 by the super talented Provençal chef, August Escoffier, in honour of Dame Nellie Melba, the Australian opera diva.

1 ½ litres water

2 cups caster sugar

½ vanilla pod, split open lengthwise

thinly peeled zest of about ⅔ of a lemon

6 just ripe peaches, washed

1 litre good quality vanilla ice-cream

40 g toasted flaked almonds

a little icing sugar for dusting

Raspberry Sauce

300 g raspberries, fresh or frozen

juice of 1 lemon

juice of 1 orange

3 tablespoons caster sugar

Combine the water, sugar, vanilla and lemon zest in a medium saucepan. Bring to a simmer and cook for 5 minutes.

Gently drop the peaches into the syrup. Bring to a slow simmer and poach the peaches for 10 minutes until they are just tender. Tip into a bowl and leave to cool. Once cold, refrigerate until 10 minutes before serving.

To make the raspberry sauce, blend all the ingredients to a purée. Strain through a fine sieve and refrigerate until ready to use.

When ready to serve, lift the peaches out of the syrup and peel them carefully. Place 6 scoops of ice-cream in a deep serving dish. Gently place the peeled peaches on top and spoon the raspberry sauce over the top. Sprinkle with toasted flaked almonds, dust with icing sugar and serve immediately. You can also serve the Pêche Melba in individual bowls.

Serves 6

RASPBERRY TRIFLES

Verrine aux framboises
From The Loire Valley Region

*The Loire Valley is known as the garden of France and red fruits are a speciality.
The climate is so pleasant that the kings of France and their entourage chose to spend
their summer holidays there. They built many stunning châteaux which are now the
pride of the region.*

Custard
250 ml milk
½ vanilla pod,
　split open lengthwise
2 egg yolks
50 g caster sugar
25 g plain flour, sifted

2 oranges
2 tablespoons Cointreau
300 ml whipped cream
6 sponge finger biscuits,
　cut in half
600 g raspberries
a little icing sugar

To make the custard, heat the milk and vanilla pod in a saucepan.

In a bowl, whisk the egg yolks with the caster sugar until well combined.
Gently stir in the flour. Pour on the hot milk and whisk well until smooth.

Return the mixture to the rinsed-out saucepan and cook over a medium heat,
whisking constantly, until the mixture begins to thicken. Tip into a bowl, whisk
briefly and leave to cool. When cold, cover with plastic film and refrigerate.

Use a sharp serrated knife to slice away the skin from the oranges, cutting right
down to the flesh. Cut the oranges into 5 mm slices and lay them in a bowl.
Drizzle with the Cointreau.

Fold the whipped cream into the cold custard, then spoon into a piping bag
without a nozzle. Pipe a little custard cream into six serving glasses. Top with a
piece of biscuit, then with 2 slices of orange and a few raspberries. Pipe on a little
more custard cream and finish with another biscuit and a few more raspberries.
Dust with icing sugar and serve.

Serves 6

SUMMER FRUIT MOUSSE

Mousse de fruits d'été

From The Loire Valley Region

This is a lovely delicate dinner party dessert. You will need to have some cooking experience and know how to use a candy thermometer. For a beautiful presentation, you will also need 4 x 10 cm PVC rings.

juice of 1 lemon	2 egg whites
juice of ½ orange	a pinch of cream of tartar
150 g raspberries,	120 ml whipped cream
⅓ vanilla pod, cut open	100 g raspberries to serve
2 leaves gelatine	100 g blackberries to serve
100 g caster sugar	100 g strawberries to serve
30 ml cold water	icing sugar for dusting

Combine the lemon and orange juice, raspberries and vanilla pod in a small saucepan and bring to the boil. Boil for 5 minutes then strain through a fine sieve into a bowl. Set aside until required.

Soak the gelatine leaves in a bowl of cold water for 5–10 minutes. Squeeze the gelatine leaves to remove excess water then stir into the raspberry juice to dissolve. Set aside to cool.

Combine the sugar and water in a saucepan and bring to a simmer. Place a candy thermometer in the pan and cook until the syrup reaches nearly 120°C. Just before the syrup reaches temperature, combine the egg whites and cream of tartar in an electric mixer and whisk to stiff peaks. With the motor running, slowly drizzle in the hot syrup. Continue whisking at a low speed for about 8 minutes, or until cool. Use a large spoon to carefully fold in the cold raspberry juice and then the whipped cream.

Arrange the PVC rings on dessert plates. Spoon the mousse mixture into the rings, smooth the surface and refrigerate for at least 2 hours to set.

To serve, carefully run a knife blade around the inside of the rings. Top each mousse with a mixture of the berries and dust with icing sugar. Carefully lift the rings away. It looks spectacular!

Serves 4

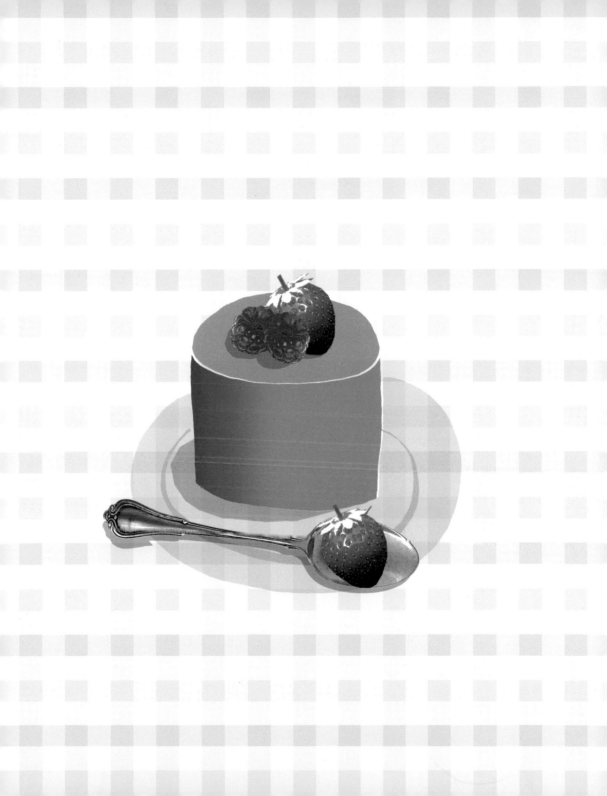

COGNAC AND GLACÉ FRUIT ICE-CREAM

Glace plombières au Cognac
From the South-West Region around Cognac

*One of my favourite tools in the kitchen is my ice-cream maker which allows me
to prepare this dessert that is to die for. Once the ice-cream is made, the dessert is
frozen in a chilled mould (I like to use an attractive cake or jelly mould) and it looks
spectacular when it is turned out. It can be made up to 3 days ahead of time.*

½ cup mixed glacé fruit,
 diced
2 tablespoons Cognac
500 ml milk
¼ vanilla bean,
 split open lengthwise

½ cup almond meal
4 egg yolks
150 g caster sugar
250 ml whipped cream
1 kg mixed summer berries

Place the glacé fruits in a bowl with the Cognac and macerate for at least
20 minutes, or overnight if you wish.

Gently heat the milk, vanilla bean and almond meal in a large saucepan.

Place the egg yolks and caster sugar in the bowl of an electric mixer and beat
for about 5 minutes until pale and creamy. Pour on the warm milk, whisking
well. Return the mixture to the rinsed-out saucepan. Cook over a medium
heat, stirring in a figure eight motion with a wooden spoon. Once the mixture
thickens to coat the back of the spoon remove the pan from the heat. Strain
through a fine sieve and discard the almond meal. Whisk the custard briefly and
leave to cool.

Tip the custard into an ice-cream machine and churn according to the
manufacturer's instructions. When the ice-cream is quite firm, add the
macerated fruits and churn briefly. Add the whipped cream and churn again
until well incorporated. Transfer the ice-cream to a pre-chilled 2-litre mould
and place in the freezer for at least 2 hours before serving.

When ready to serve, briefly dip the mould in warm water to loosen the ice-
cream, then invert it onto a deep serving platter. Cut into slices and serve with
seasonal berries of your choice.

Serves 6–8

NOUGAT ICE-CREAM WITH RASPBERRY SAUCE

Nougat glacé avec un coulis de framboises
From the North Provence Region

This is one of my favourite desserts, but it does require some cooking experience as you need to make a caramel and use a candy thermometer.

70 g caster sugar
1 tablespoon water
120 g hazelnuts,
  roasted and skinned
60 g honey
30 g liquid glucose
3 egg whites
a pinch of cream of tartar

150 g glacé apricots,
  cut into 1 cm squares
30 g glacé cherries,
  cut into 5 mm squares
300 ml whipped cream
Raspberry Sauce
  (page 100) to serve

Combine 40 g of the sugar with the water in a small saucepan and cook over a medium heat until it darkens to a caramel. Add the hazelnuts and stir for 2 minutes to coat them with the caramel. Very carefully tip the caramelised nuts onto a piece of lightly oiled baking paper and spread them out. When cold, separate out three-quarters of the caramelised nuts and chop them roughly. Reserve the remaining whole nuts to garnish.

Combine the honey, liquid glucose and remaining 30 g sugar in a small saucepan over a medium heat. Place a candy thermometer in the pan and cook until the syrup reaches 100°C.

Once the syrup reaches temperature, combine the egg whites and cream of tartar in an electric mixer and whisk to stiff peaks.

Continue cooking the syrup until it reaches 120ºC then slowly drizzle it onto the egg whites, whisking continuously. Continue whisking at a low speed for about 10 minutes. Transfer the ice-cream mixture to the refrigerator for 10 minutes to cool.

Carefully fold the chopped hazelnuts and glacé fruits into the cooled ice-cream mixture. Fold in the whipped cream then tip into a 22 cm cake tin lined with plastic film. Cover the surface and freeze for at least 6 hours.

When ready to serve, dip the mould briefly in warm water to loosen the ice-cream, then invert it onto a serving dish. Peel away the plastic film and cut into slices. Top with caramelised nuts and serve with the raspberry sauce.

Serves 8–10

Fraisier

Framboisine

Meringue chocolaté

HAZELNUT MERINGUE WITH CHESTNUT CREAM AND RASPBERRIES

Méringue aux noisettes et crème de marrons avec framboises
From The Alps Region

A French cousin of the pavlova, this dessert uses sweetened chestnut cream which has a lovely strong flavour and contrasts wonderfully with the meringue and fresh raspberries.

30 g hazelnut meal
90 g caster sugar
½ tablespoon cornflour
2 egg whites
a pinch of cream of tartar
¼ teaspoon white vinegar
200 ml cream

100 g crème de marrons
　(sweetened chestnut cream, which
　is available from delicatessens)
450 g raspberries
¼ cup apricot jam
2 teaspoons water
a little icing sugar for dusting

Preheat the oven to 180°C. Line a flat baking sheet with baking paper and draw a 25 cm circle on the paper.

Place the hazelnut meal in a small frying pan over a medium heat and toast until lightly browned. Mix with half the caster sugar and the cornflour.

Place the egg whites and cream of tartar in the bowl of an electric mixer and whisk to medium-stiff peaks. With the motor turned to low, gradually whisk in the remaining caster sugar and the vinegar, to form stiff peaks.

Fold the hazelnut mixture into the meringue then spoon into a piping bag fitted with a 1 cm round nozzle. Pipe a 25 cm spiral disc onto the prepared baking sheet, working from the outer edge in to the centre. Bake for about 25 minutes. If the meringue browns too much, reduce the oven temperature. When cooked, the meringue should be dry and firm. Remove from the oven and leave to cool.

Whip the cream, then gently fold in the crème de marrons. Spread onto the meringue and top with the raspberries.

Heat the apricot jam with the water to make a runny glaze. Brush the raspberries with the glaze. Just before serving, dust with icing sugar.

Serves 6

CHOCOLATE CONCORDE CAKE

Gâteau concorde au chocolat

From the Paris Region by Pierrick Boyer

This delicate cake was named after the Place de la Concorde in Paris. It is from this well known square that the Tour de France sprints begin every year, to finish on the Champs Elysées.

9 egg whites
220 g caster sugar
40 g Dutch cocoa,
    plus extra for dusting
150 g icing sugar, plus extra
    for dusting

200 g dark cooking chocolate,
    broken into small pieces
200 g unsalted butter,
    cut into pieces

Preheat the oven to 90°C. Line a flat baking sheet with baking paper and draw 2 x 18 cm circles on the paper.

Place 5 of the egg whites in the bowl of an electric mixer and whisk to medium-stiff peaks. Gradually whisk in 120 g of the caster sugar until well incorporated.

Mix the cocoa with the icing sugar and gently fold into the meringue mixture. Spoon into a piping bag fitted with a 1 cm round nozzle. Pipe 2 x 18 cm spiral discs onto the prepared baking sheet. Also pipe 4 x 30 cm long, thin 'sticks' of meringue. Bake for about 1 hour, then turn off the oven and leave the meringue for a further 30 minutes. Remove from the oven and leave to cool completely.

Place the chocolate and butter in a bowl set over a saucepan of medium-hot water. Stir together until smooth and well mixed. Set the bowl aside.

Meanwhile, whisk the remaining 4 egg whites to stiff peaks, then gradually whisk in the remaining 100 g caster sugar until well incorporated. Fold a little of the mixture into the melted chocolate, then gently fold in remaining egg whites until just mixed. Spoon into a piping bag.

When ready to assemble, place a 18 cm x 8 cm high cake ring on a wire rack. Place one of the chocolate meringue discs inside, trimming the edges to fit, if necessary. Pipe a 5 cm layer of chocolate mousse on top of the meringue, then place the second chocolate meringue disc on top. Spread with a thin layer of chocolate mousse then transfer the cake to the freezer for about 20 minutes to set.

Transfer the cake onto a serving plate and carefully lift away the cake ring. Break the thin meringue sticks into 3–4 cm pieces and stick them all over the sides and top of the cake. Take your time. The effect is stunning. Dust with a little icing sugar and cocoa powder.

Serves 8

RASPBERRY ICE-CREAM CAKE WITH MERINGUE

Vacherin aux framboises
From the Alsace Region

The region of Alsace is famous for this ice-cream dessert, which combines fruit sorbet and vanilla ice-cream, served with home-made meringues and whipped cream. It's one of my favourite desserts after a special dinner.

To assemble the vacherin, you will need a 2-litre charlotte mould that should be well-chilled in the freezer. Once the mould is filled, transfer to the freezer for a minimum of 1 hour before serving, so that it sets very firm.

Raspberry Sorbet
500 g raspberries
1 ½ cups sugar
juice of 1 lemon
juice of 2 oranges

Meringues
whites of 3 x 61 g eggs
a pinch of cream of tartar
120 g caster sugar
50 g pure icing sugar, sifted

1 litre good quality vanilla
  ice-cream
300 ml whipped cream
300 g raspberries

To make the raspberry sorbet, combine the raspberries, sugar, lemon and orange in a food processor and blend to a purée. Strain through a fine sieve, then transfer to an ice-cream machine and churn according to the manufacturer's instructions. When the sorbet is ready, transfer it to a pre-chilled container and place in the freezer.

If you don't have an ice-cream maker, freeze the mixture in a stainless-steel bowl. When it starts to freeze, whisk for 10–15 seconds and return to freezer. Repeat at regular intervals until it becomes too firm to whisk. The whisking lightens the sorbet and prevents large ice crystals from forming.

To make the meringues, preheat the oven to 140°C. Line a baking sheet with baking paper.

Place the egg whites and cream of tartar in the bowl of an electric mixer and whisk to soft peaks. Gradually whisk in half of the sugar until the meringue becomes shiny and stiffer. Whisk in the remaining sugar and the icing sugar until well incorporated.

Spoon 12 oval spoonfuls of meringue on the baking sheet, leaving a little space in between each one. Don't worry if the shapes are not perfect and avoid fiddling with them. Cook for 20 minutes then reduce the oven temperature to 100ºC and cook for a further 60 minutes. Turn off the oven and leave the meringues for a further hour to dry completely. Store in an airtight container.

To assemble the vacherin, spoon the vanilla ice-cream into a chilled charlotte mould. Smooth the surface then top with the raspberry sorbet. Freeze for at least 1 hour to set well.

To unmould the vacherin, briefly dip the mould in warm water to loosen the ice-cream, then invert it onto a serving dish. Stick meringues around the sides of the ice-cream using a little whipped cream to attach them. Use as many meringues as necessary. Spoon the whipped cream into a piping bag fitted with a fluted nozzle and use to pipe rosettes of whipped cream in-between the meringues. Top with raspberries.

Use a sharp knife to cut the vacherin into slices, so that everyone gets a meringue.

Serves 8–10

CHESTNUT CAKE

Gâteau aux marrons

From the Languedoc Region by Sébastien Burot

You find lovely layered cakes such as this in many French pâtisseries and they make wonderful desserts for special occasions. To create a great-looking cake you will need to assemble it in a cake ring that is the same size as your sponge cake. You can decorate it with chocolate curls, glacé chestnuts and even gold leaves.

Rum Syrup
120 ml water
120 g caster sugar
40 ml rum

Cake
200 g unsweetened purée de
   marrons (chestnut purée, which
   is available from delicatessens)
350 g Crème Pâtissière (see page 130)
300 ml whipped cream
1 x 18 cm plain or chocolate
   sponge cake

Chocolate Icing
80 ml cream
3 tablespoons Rum Syrup
200 g dark cooking
   chocolate, cut into
   small pieces

To make the rum syrup, combine the water and sugar in a saucepan. Bring to a simmer and cook for 5 minutes. Stir in the rum and allow to cool before refrigerating until ready to use.

Beat the chestnut purée and crème pâtissière until well combined. Fold in the whipped cream.

When ready to assemble, place the cake ring on a wire rack. Cut the sponge cake horizontally into 3 even layers and if necessary, trim them to fit into the cake ring. Place a layer of sponge cake into the base of the cake ring. Brush with a little rum syrup then spoon half the chestnut cream on top and smooth the surface. Top with another layer of sponge cake and brush with a little more syrup. Spoon in the remaining chestnut cream. Brush one side of the remaining sponge layer with syrup and place that side on top of the cream. Transfer the cake, still on the rack, to the freezer for 30 minutes to set.

While the cake is setting, make the icing. Combine the cream and rum syrup in a saucepan and bring to the boil. Stir in the chocolate until melted. Remove from heat and leave to cool slightly, stirring from time to time to keep it smooth.

Transfer the cake onto a serving plate and carefully lift away the cake ring. Use a flat spatula to glaze the cake all over with chocolate icing. Place in refrigerator to allow the icing to set.

Serves 8–10

STRAWBERRY SPONGE CAKE

Gâteau fraisier

From the Languedoc-Roussillon Region by Pierrick Boyer

Many of the sweetest French strawberries are grown in the sunny region of Languedoc-Roussillon, and this gâteau is popular in the pâtisseries of the region and, naturellement, in the top pastry shops in Paris.

To make this exquisite cake you will need to be an experienced pastry cook and for perfect presentation you will need a few pieces of special equipment, such as a cake ring and acetate plastic. Both are available from specialist food stores.

Syrup
30 g caster sugar
30 ml water

Custard Filling
3 gelatine leaves
400 ml milk
1 vanilla pod, split
    open lengthwise
50 g caster sugar
50 g cornflour
2 whole eggs

100 g butter, cut into cubes
400 ml whipped cream

Cake
1 x 22 cm plain sponge cake
500 g medium–large
    strawberries, halved
a little icing sugar for dusting
250 g marzipan
a few raspberries and
    strawberries to serve
150 ml whipped cream to serve

To make the syrup, combine the water and sugar in a saucepan. Bring to a simmer and cook for 2 minutes to make a syrup. Set aside to cool.

To make the custard, first soak the gelatine leaves in a bowl of cold water for 5–10 minutes.

Combine the milk and vanilla pod in a saucepan and bring almost to the boil.

In a bowl, whisk the eggs with the sugar and cornflour until well blended. Pour on the hot milk and whisk well until smooth. Return the mixture to the rinsed-out saucepan and cook over a medium heat, whisking constantly, until the mixture thickens. Tip the mixture into a bowl, whisk briefly and leave to cool a little.

Squeeze the gelatine leaves to remove excess water then stir into the custard to dissolve. Whisk in the butter cubes until melted and smooth. Pour the custard into a tray so that it can cool quickly, but don't allow it to set firm. When the custard is cold, fold in the whipped cream. Transfer the custard to a piping bag fitted with a 1 cm round nozzle.

When ready to assemble the cake, line the base and sides of a 22 cm cake ring with plastic acetate, which stops the cake sticking. Place the cake ring on a baking sheet lined with baking paper.

Cut the sponge cake horizontally to create 2 x 1 ½ cm layers. Trim 1 cm from the edge of each, so they are smaller than the cake ring. Place one of the sponge layers in the base of the cake ring. Pipe custard into the space between the sponge and the sides of the ring. Stick strawberry halves into the custard around the edge of the ring, with the flat edges facing outwards.

Pipe a layer of custard on top of the sponge and in-between the strawberries. Use a small palette knife to spread the custard up the sides of the cake ring to the top. Arrange a layer of strawberry halves on top of the custard then sit the second layer of sponge cake on top. Brush with the flavoured sugar syrup. Finish with a layer of custard, smooth the surface and refrigerate for 2 hours to set.

Dust your work surface with a little icing sugar. Roll the marzipan out thinly and cut out a 22 cm circle. Lift it carefully onto the top of the set cake.

Transfer the cake to a cake stand and very carefully lift away the cake ring. Decorate the cake with a few strawberries or raspberries and dust with icing sugar. Just before serving, remove the strip of acetate from the side of the cake. Cut into slices and serve with whipped cream.

Serves 8

CHERRY MOUSSE CAKE

Charlotte aux cerises

From the Alsace/Franche Comté Region

In the lovely green region of South Alsace and North Franche Comté the sides of the road are often lined with cherry groves, and cherries feature in many local desserts, as well as being transformed into a superb cherry liqueur. For this dessert, which is like a sort of French trifle, I use a loaf tin as a mould.

Custard Filling
2 gelatine leaves
500 ml milk
½ vanilla pod,
   split open lengthwise
5 egg yolks
150 g caster sugar

1 x 25 cm square sponge cake,
   about 4 cm thick
300 ml whipped cream
600 g cherries, stoned at the
   last moment
Raspberry Sauce (page 100)
   to serve (optional)

To make the custard, first soak the gelatine leaves in a bowl of cold water for 5–10 minutes.

Combine the milk and vanilla pod in a saucepan and heat until nearly boiling.

In a bowl whisk the egg yolks with the sugar until light and creamy – it takes at least 5 minutes. Pour on the hot milk and whisk well until smooth. Return the mixture to the rinsed-out saucepan and cook over a medium heat, stirring with a wooden spoon until the custard lightly coats the back of the spoon. Strain the custard into a bowl and leave it to cool slightly.

Squeeze the gelatine leaves to remove excess water then stir into the warm custard to dissolve. Transfer to the fridge to cool for 20–30 minutes, but check to ensure the custard does not set.

Line a loaf tin with baking paper. Cut the sponge cake horizontally into 3 layers, then cut the layers into pieces and use to line the base and sides of the tin.

Fold the whipped cream into the cold custard. Pour a little custard over the sponge pieces, to about one-third of the way up the tin. Top with the stoned cherries to almost fill the tin.

Add more custard, then tap the tin lightly to help the ingredients to settle. Add more custard to fill the tin. Cover with a layer of sponge pieces to form a lid. Carefully wrap the tin in plastic film and refrigerate for at least 4 hours to set.

When ready to serve, carefully remove the plastic film and unmould the cake. Use a very sharp knife to cut into about 10 thick slices and serve with raspberry sauce, if you wish.

Serves 8–10

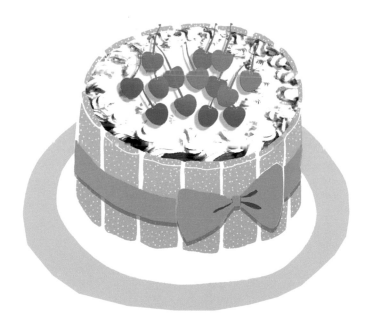

CHERRY CLAFOUTIS

Clafoutis aux cerises

From the Limousin Region by Elisabeth Kerdelhué

A clafoutis is a traditional French dessert in which fresh fruit – usually cherries – are baked in a batter. It is rather like a fruit flan without the pastry. In France many people have cherry trees in their back yard – we had several at our home – and the fruit is used in desserts like this one.

700 g cherries, stoned
40 g plain flour, sifted
60 g caster sugar
a pinch of salt
4 eggs

600 ml full-cream milk
2 egg yolks
2 tablespoons Cognac or Kirsch
a little icing sugar for dusting

Preheat oven to 180°C. Lightly butter a 28 cm x 3 cm deep porcelain flan dish. Arrange the cherries over the base.

Combine the sifted flour, sugar, salt and 2 of the eggs in a bowl and mix together well. Add a little milk and mix well. Mix in the 2 remaining whole eggs and the egg yolks. Lastly, mix in the remaining milk.

Carefully strain the mixture into the flan dish over the cherries. Drizzle the Cognac evenly over the top. Carefully place in the oven and bake for about 45 minutes.

Remove from the oven and dust with icing sugar before serving. Take care as it is very hot.

Serves 8

APPLE TART FLAMED WITH CALVADOS

Tarte aux pommes flambée au Calvados

From the Normandy Region by Angie Gaté

Normandy is famous for its cream, apples and a beautiful apple liqueur called Calvados, and these three special ingredients blend together perfectly in this lovely apple tart.

8 apples (Red Delicious,
    Granny Smith or another
    variety of your choice)
2 tablespoons water
250 g puff pastry

1 egg yolk
1 tablespoon water
2 tablespoons cream
2 tablespoons caster sugar
3 tablespoons Calvados

Preheat the oven to 200°C. Line a baking sheet with baking paper.

Peel 4 of the apples, then cut them into eighths and remove the cores. Cook with 2 tablespoons of water in a covered saucepan until tender. Mash the apple to a purée and leave to cool.

Roll out the pastry on a floured surface to a 28 cm square, about 3 mm thick.

Carefully lift the pastry onto the prepared baking sheet. Prick the pastry with a fork to prevent shrinkage, then cut out a 28 cm circle. Use the tip of a knife blade to trace a smaller circle on the pastry, leaving a 2 cm edge. Mix the egg yolk and water together to make eggwash and use to brush the edge.

Spread a layer of apple purée over the centre of the pastry, leaving the edge free. Spread the cream over the purée.

Peel, quarter and core the remaining apples and cut each quarter into 4 segments. Starting at the outer edge, arrange the apple segments on top of the purée, forming a circular spiral towards the centre. Overlapp the slices a little and make sure you leave no gaps.

Sprinkle on the sugar and bake for about 20 minutes. Then reduce the oven temperature to 150°C and bake for a further 30 minutes. The tart is cooked when the pastry is golden brown and crisp and the edges of the apples are lightly browned. The pastry base should be dry and lightly browned.

Carefully transfer the tart to a serving platter.

Heat the Calvados in a small saucepan and bring to the boil. Remove the pan from the heat and flame the Calvados. (It is best to do this away from the stove.) Carefully pour the flaming liqueur over the tart and serve when the flames have subsided.

Serves 8

APPLE PIE WITH ARMAGNAC

Tarte aux pommes à l'Armagnac
From the North Pyrenees Region

The Armagnac in this pie makes a difference, but you could also use brandy or a liqueur such as Drambuie or Kirsch. It's a delicious rustic dessert and is also perfect for afternoon tea.

4 dried figs, cut into
  1 cm cubes
30 ml Armagnac
1 tablespoon finely
  grated lemon zest
20 g butter
60 g caster sugar

4 apples, peeled, cored
  and cut into 1 cm rings
1 egg yolk
1 teaspoon water
2 x 22 cm squares rolled puff pastry
250 g pure cream to serve

Place the fig pieces in a bowl with the Armagnac and lemon zest and macerate for at least 1 hour or overnight.

Melt the butter in a large non-stick frying pan over a medium heat. Add the sugar and when it has melted add the apple slices. Cook until the apple slices have caramelised on one side, then turn and caramelise the other side. Add the figs and Armagnac to the pan and stir in. Flame for a few seconds. (It is best to do this away from the stove.) Transfer the apples to a shallow dish and leave to cool.

Lightly grease a 22 cm loose-bottomed flan tin. Mix the egg yolk and water together to make eggwash.

Place the pastry squares on a floured bench and cut out 2 circles to the size of the flan tin. Lay one pastry circle in the tin and brush the edges with the eggwash. Arrange the cold apple in the centre of the pastry, leaving an edge of about 2 cm.

Carefully place the second pastry circle on top and pinch the edges together to seal. Use the tip of a knife blade to make a hole in the centre of the pastry and brush with eggwash. Make a criss-cross pattern on the pastry using the prongs of a fork. Place the tart in the refrigerator for 15 minutes.

Preheat the oven to 180°C.

Bake the tart for about 30 minutes, or until the pastry is cooked and golden brown. Allow to cool slightly before carefully removing from the tin. Cut the tart into wedges and serve with cream.

Serves 8

PRUNE AND PEAR FLAN

Flan aux pruneaux et aux poires

From the Brittany Region by Pierrick Boyer

Almost every French bakery and pastry shop sells one or several varieties of this classic tart from Brittany. With their pastry base, baked custard and fruit filling they are a firm family favourite – and children love them.

1 x 25 cm square sheet
   puff pastry
200 g caster sugar
40 g plain flour, sifted
4 eggs
250 ml thickened cream

250 ml milk
1 large or 2 small poached pears,
   cored and cut into thin slices
6 prunes, cut into small pieces
a little icing sugar for dusting

Preheat the oven to 180°C. Grease an 18 cm loose-bottomed flan tin and arrange it on a flat baking sheet.

Carefully lift the pastry onto the prepared flan tin, pushing it in gently. Don't trim the edges as the pastry may shrink in the oven. Arrange a sheet of baking paper on top of the pastry and fill with rice. Bake for 10–15 minutes or until the pastry is just cooked. Remove the paper and rice.

In a bowl mix the caster sugar with the flour. Beat in 2 of the eggs until smooth. Beat in the remaining 2 eggs, followed by the cream and milk to form a smooth custard.

Arrange the pears and prunes in the tart shell then carefully pour in the custard. (Any leftover custard can be baked separately in an oven-proof porcelain dish.) Bake for 15–20 minutes until set and beginning to brown.

Trim the edges of the pastry. Remove the flan from the tin and transfer it to a cake stand or serving plate. Dust with icing sugar just before serving.

Serves 8

Note: You can decorate the cooked flan with extra pears and prunes if you wish.

PLUM TART

Tarte aux prunes

From The Alps Region by Michael Gaté

The Alpine region is famous for its wonderful fruit tarts, prepared throughout summer and autumn with local fruits and a dash of liqueur made from the same fruit.

The sweet shortcrust pastry is my favourite for sweet tarts and pies, with the almonds providing a pleasant crunch. The pastry needs time to rest, so you will need to make it at least 1 hour before using.

Sweet Shortcrust Pastry
50 g whole blanched almonds
150 g unsalted butter, cubed
1 x 61 g egg
2 drops pure vanilla essence
a pinch of salt
100 g icing sugar
250 g plain flour

80 g sugar
80 g butter
1 whole egg
1 egg yolk
2 tablespoons plum liqueur (or
   use Kirsch, Pear William, brandy)
80 g almond meal
1 tablespoon plain flour, sifted
8 large plums, halved and stoned
   (blood plums are lovely)
a little icing sugar for dusting

To make the sweet shortcrust pastry, place the almonds in a food processor and chop coarsely but evenly. Add the butter, egg, vanilla and salt and process briefly until the butter has softened slightly. Continue to blend, gradually adding the icing sugar and flour until the pastry is well mixed. Tip out the pastry and use your hands to shape it into a ball. Wrap in plastic film or foil. Flatten slightly and refrigerate for at least 1 hour before using.

Preheat the oven to 200°C. Grease a 25 cm square or a 28 cm round flan tin and place it on a flat baking sheet.

Combine the sugar and butter in a small food processor and blend until well combined and creamy. Add the egg and egg yolk and blend. Add the liqueur, then the almond meal and plain flour, and blend until combined. Transfer the almond cream to a bowl.

Remove the pastry from the fridge and knead slightly to soften. Lightly flour 2 x 30 cm squares of baking paper. Place the pastry between them and roll out to a thickness of around 3 mm. Carefully lift the pastry onto the prepared flan tin, pushing it in gently. Don't trim the edges as the pastry may shrink in the oven.

Spread the almond cream over the pastry base and up the sides. Arrange the plum halves, skin-side down, on top, working from the edge to the centre. Bake for 20 minutes then trim the pastry edges neatly.

Reduce the oven temperature to 150°C and bake for a further 35–40 minutes or until the pastry base is dry and lightly browned. Just before serving, dust the tart with icing sugar.

Serves 6–8

RASPBERRY TARTLETS

Tartelettes aux framboises
From The Loire Valley Region

I prepared this dessert hundreds of times during my chef's apprenticeship in the Loire Valley. The pastry shells and crème pâtissière can both be made ahead of time, but if you make the pastry on the same day, be sure to allow time for it to rest for at least 1 hour before rolling out. Avoid assembling the tartlets more than 2 hours before serving as the pastry will become soggy.

Crème Pâtissière
250 ml milk
2 egg yolks
⅓ vanilla pod, split
   open lengthwise
50 g caster sugar
25 g plain flour, sifted

Sweet Shortcrust Pastry
   (page 128), chilled
3 tablespoons pure cream
3 tablespoons apricot jam
splash of water
600 g raspberries

To make the crème pâtissière bring the milk to a boil in a medium saucepan.

In a bowl, whisk the egg yolks, vanilla pod and caster sugar for 2 minutes. When well blended, whisk in the sifted flour. Pour on the hot milk and whisk well until smooth.

Return the mixture to the rinsed-out saucepan and cook over a medium heat, whisking constantly, until the mixture thickens and comes to a boil. Once it reaches a boil, tip the mixture into a bowl. Whisk briefly and leave to cool. When cold, remove the vanilla pod, cover with plastic film and refrigerate until ready to use.

When ready to make the tartlets, preheat the oven to 200°C. Grease 6 cm loose-bottomed tartlet tins and arrange them on a flat baking sheet.

Remove the pastry from the fridge and knead slightly before rolling it out on a well-floured surface.

Roll out the pastry on a well-floured surface and cut into squares to fit the tartlet moulds. Line the moulds with the pastry, pushing it in gently. Trim the edges with your fingertips, taking care not to make them too thin and fragile. Cook for around 10 minutes, or until the edges have browned and the pastry is cooked. Remove from the oven and leave to cool before unmoulding.

Mix the crème patissière with the cream.

Heat the apricot jam with a little water to make a runny glaze.

To assemble the tartlets, place a spoonful of pastry cream into each pastry shell and spread it a little. Arrange the raspberries decoratively over the cream, working from the edge to the centre. Brush lightly with the apricot glaze and chill until ready to serve.

Makes about 20 x 6 cm tartlets

MONT BLANC CHESTNUT CAKES

Petits gâteaux Mont Blanc

From The Alps Region by Pierrick Boyer

The French are mad about chestnuts and this dessert, using a luscious chestnut cream, was created to celebrate the beauty of the alpine Mont Blanc peak. You need special pastry equipment, in particular a piping bag fitted with a Mont Blanc nozzle.

250 g Sweet Shortcrust Pastry
  (page 128)
50 g almond meal
50 g icing sugar, plus extra
  for dusting
50 g plain flour, sifted
50 g softened butter
1 egg
6 teaspoons orange marmalade

6 small meringues, the size of
  a ball of cotton wool
100 g sweet chestnut cream
  (crème de marrons, which is
  available from delicatessens)
100 g unsweetened chestnut purée
  (purée de marrons, which is
  available from delicatessens)
100 ml whipped cream

Preheat the oven to 170°C. Lightly grease 6 x 6 cm tartlet rings. Arrange the rings on a flat baking sheet.

Roll the sweet pastry out to a thickness of 3 mm. Cut out 6 x 10 cm discs of pastry and use to line the tartlet rings, pushing the pastry in gently. Trim the edges neatly.

In a mixing bowl, combine the almond meal, icing sugar, plain flour and butter. Add the egg and mix until smooth. Spoon into a piping bag and neatly fill the pastry cases so they are three-quarters full. Bake for about 15 minutes or until the pastry is cooked and golden brown. Remove from the oven and leave to cool before turning the tartlets out.

Spread 1 teaspoon of orange marmalade on each tartlet, and top with a small meringue.

In a bowl combine the chestnut cream with the chestnut purée. Spoon the mixture into a piping bag fitted with a special Mont Blanc nozzle and use it to pipe the traditional vermicelli-like icing over the top of the meringues to cover them well. Dust with icing sugar. Use a piping bag, fitted with a star nozzle, to pipe cream rosettes of 'snow' on the summit of your mini Mont Blanc cakes. Refrigerate until 10 minutes before serving.

Makes 6 little cakes

PUFF PASTRY AND ALMOND CREAM CAKE

Pithiviers

From The Loire Valley Region by Sébastien Burot

This classic cake is also known as Galette des Rois and it is really popular on 6th January, when French Catholics celebrate the Epiphany – the arrival of the Three Wise Kings. The Kings' cake is usually purchased from the local pâtisserie.

Almond Cream
125 g butter
125 g caster sugar
2 eggs
125 g almond meal
30 ml rum
25 g plain flour

2 x 25 cm square sheets
   puff pastry
   (or 500 g puff pastry)
1 egg yolk
2 tablespoons water

Preheat the oven to 220°C. Line a flat baking sheet with baking paper.

To make the almond cream, combine the butter and sugar in the bowl of an electric mixer and beat until well combined. Add the eggs one at a time, mixing well after each addition. Add the almond meal and mix well. Add the rum and flour and mix well. Spoon the mixture into a piping bag without a nozzle.

Lay the pastry sheets out on a work surface (or roll out to a thickness of 5 mm) and cut out 2 x 25 cm rounds. A large plate serves well as a template.

Carefully lift one of the pastry rounds onto the prepared baking sheet lined with baking paper. Use the tip of a knife blade to trace a smaller circle, around 16 cm in diameter, on the pastry round.

Mix the egg yolk and water together to make eggwash and use to brush the outer edge of the pastry. Pipe a generous mound of almond cream in the centre. Cover with a second pastry disc and press the edges together to seal. Brush with more eggwash. Use the blade of a small knife to mark the surface with curved lines that radiate from the centre of the dome to the edges in an attractive pattern.

Bake for 15 minutes, then reduce the oven temperature to 200°C and bake for a further 20–25 minutes, or until the cake is browned underneath.

Serves 6–8

PARIS BREST GÂTEAU

From the Paris Region by Philippe Mouchel

Named after a bicycle race from, you guessed it, Paris to Brest, this delicious French gâteau is made by most traditional French pâtissiers and is often available in individual portions. You can prepare both the crème pâtissière pralinée and the choux pastry rings the day before you serve the dessert.

Crème Pâtissière Pralinée
60 g butter
50 g hazelnut pralinée or
   chocolate pralinée (or use Nuttella)
Crème Pâtissière (page 130), chilled

Choux Pastry
100 ml water
150 ml milk
½ teaspoon salt

10 g sugar
80 g butter, cut into small pieces
150 g plain flour, sifted
4 eggs
1 egg yolk
1 teaspoon water
about 50 g flaked almonds
icing sugar for dusting

To make the crème pâtissière pralinée, beat the butter with the hazelnut pralinée until well combined. Add the crème pâtissière and mix well to combine. Refrigerate until ready to use.

Preheat the oven to 205°C. Place a 20 cm flan ring on a baking sheet lined with baking paper.

To make the choux pastry, combine the water, milk, salt, sugar and butter in a medium saucepan and bring to a simmer. When the butter has dissolved, lower the heat and add the flour in one go, stirring vigorously with a wooden spoon for a few minutes until it forms a smooth mass.

Transfer the mixture to the bowl of an electric mixer and mix on medium speed with the K beater. Add the eggs one at a time, mixing well after each addition, until the dough is smooth. Spoon into a large piping bag fitted with a 1 cm nozzle.

Pipe a circle of dough inside the flan ring close to the edge. Pipe a second circle inside the first one then pipe a third circle on top of these two circles.

Mix the egg yolk and water together to make eggwash and brush over the pastry. Sprinkle on the flaked almonds and bake for 20 minutes. Reduce the oven temperature to 150ºC and bake for a further 25 minutes. Turn off the oven and leave the pastry in the oven to dry for about 1 hour. Remove from the oven and leave on a wire rack until completely cold. Carefully lift away the flan ring.

When nearly ready to serve, spoon the chilled crème pâtissière pralinée into a piping bag fitted with a serrated nozzle. Split the pastry in half horizontally and fill the base to a height of about 2 cm. Gently place the pastry lid on top. Dust with icing sugar and serve straight away. Alternatively, store in the refrigerator until 10 minutes before serving.

Serves 8

ST HONORÉ CAKE

Gâteau St. Honoré

Popular all over France by Pierrick Boyer

*Pierrick Boyer, our team's talented pâtissier, prepared this popular and delicious
French gâteau to celebrate Bastille day, the French national day on the 14th July.
It is a rather elaborate cake and to make it you will need good baking skills and some
specialist equipment, such as a special St Honoré nozzle.*

250 ml water
100 g butter
a pinch of salt
160 g plain flour, sifted
5 x 60 g eggs
1 x 20 cm square rolled puff pastry
200 g fondant (available from
  specialist food stores)

250 g glucose syrup
300 g Crème Patissière
  (page 130)
300 g whipped cream
a few halved strawberries
icing sugar for dusting

Preheat the oven to 180°C. Line 2 baking sheets with baking paper.

Combine the water, butter and salt in a medium saucepan and bring to a
simmer. When the butter has dissolved, lower the heat and add the flour in one
go, stirring vigorously with a wooden spoon for a few minutes until it forms a
smooth mass.

Transfer the mixture to the bowl of an electric mixer and mix on medium speed
with the K beater. Add the eggs one at a time, mixing well after each addition,
until the dough is smooth. Spoon into a large piping bag fitted with a 1 cm
nozzle.

Place the puff pastry square on a floured surface and cut out a 20 cm disc. Lift
it carefully onto the prepared baking sheet. Pipe a circle of choux pastry around
the edge of the puff pastry disc. Now pipe a loose spiral shape, starting from the
centre and working to the edge.

Pipe 12 x 3 cm choux puffs onto the second prepared baking sheet. Place both trays in the oven and cook for about 20 minutes, until the pastries are golden brown and cooked. Remove from the oven and cool the cake and choux puffs on a wire rack.

Place the fondant and glucose syrup in a small saucepan. Bring to the boil and cook to a caramel. Very carefully dip the choux puffs into the hot caramel then place them, caramel side down, on a non-stick baking tray to cool. When cold they will have a nice smooth caramel edge.

Dip the opposite sides of the choux puffs into the caramel, then stick them onto the cake, in a circle around the edge, so the flat caramel sides are uppermost. Make sure you set one choux puff aside.

In a bowl fold the crème pâtissière with the whipped cream and spoon it into a piping bag fitted with a special St Honoré nozzle. Pipe a generous amount into the centre of the cake forming the traditional little rounded peaks. (If you don't have a special nozzle, pipe it in as attractively as you can.)

Using a serrated knife, slice the choux puffs in half horizontally and remove the caramelised lids. Carefully fill the choux halves that are attached to the cake, then replace the lids. Place the reserved choux puff in the centre of the cake. As a final flourish, decorate the top with strawberry halves and dust with icing sugar.

Serves 8

SAVOIE SPONGE CAKE

Gâteau de Savoie

From The Alps Region

My grandmother, who inspired me to become a chef, baked one of these lovely gâteaux each time we had a special family celebration. I love to serve it with a runny custard and fresh fruits.

90 g plain flour
90 g cornflour
6 eggs, separated
grated zest of 1 lemon

300 g caster sugar
a pinch of cream of tartar
icing sugar for dusting

Preheat the oven to 180°C. Butter a 25 cm round cake tin.

Sift the plain flour and the cornflour together.

Place the egg yolks, lemon zest and 150 g of caster sugar in the bowl of an electric mixer and beat until very pale and mousse-like.

Add the cream of tartar to the egg whites and whisk them to stiff peaks. Gradually whisk in the remaining 150 g caster sugar, until well incorporated. Gently fold the egg whites into the egg yolks. Lastly, fold in the sifted flours, being careful not to over-mix.

Pour the cake mixture into the prepared tin and smooth the surface. Dust with a little icing sugar and bake for 35–40 minutes. Remove from the oven and cool for about 10 minutes on a wire rack. Turn out of the tin and cool completely before serving.

Serves 10–12

WALNUT CAKE

Gâteau aux noix
From The Alps Region

This family cake is very popular in the region of Grenoble, famous for its large production of walnuts.

Cake
160 g fresh walnuts
150 g butter
140 g sugar
finely grated zest of 1 lemon
4 eggs, separated
¾ cup dried breadcrumbs
a pinch of cream of tartar

Icing
50 ml water
100 g sugar
2 drops red wine vinegar
10 walnut halves
a little icing sugar for
  dusting

Preheat the oven to 150°C. Butter a 22 cm cake tin, line the base with baking paper, then butter the baking paper.

Place the walnuts in a food processor and grind to a coarse meal.

Combine the butter, lemon zest and half the sugar in an electric mixer and beat until pale and creamy. Add the egg yolks, one at a time, beating on medium speed. Add the breadcrumbs and chopped walnuts and mix well.

Whisk the egg whites and cream of tartar to medium-stiff peaks. Gradually whisk in the rest of the caster sugar until well incorporated. Add a third of the egg whites to the batter and fold in well. Carefully fold in the remaining whites.

Pour into the prepared cake tin and smooth the surface. Transfer to the oven and bake for 1 hour.

Remove the cake from the oven cool for 5 minutes before turning out onto a wire rack.

To make the icing, combine the water, sugar and vinegar in a small saucepan and bring to the boil. Cook to a light brown caramel. Pour the icing slowly onto the centre of the cake and use a spatula to spread it out smoothly. Garnish with walnut halves and dust the edges of the cake with icing sugar.

Serves 8–10

KOUGELHOPF GÂTEAU

From the Alsace Region by Philippe Mouchel

This wonderful yeast cake is a great speciality of Alsace. You can find it in every pâtisserie and bakery in the region and at the better hotels it is usually on offer for breakfast. You will need a special kougelhopf mould to create the traditional fluted, curved shape.

100 g raisins
50 ml rum
12 g fresh yeast
60 ml milk, boiled
   and cooled to lukewarm
250 g plain flour
40 g caster sugar
1 teaspoon salt
4 eggs

180 g butter at room temperature,
   plus extra for greasing
20 g extra butter to butter
   kugelhopf mould
100 g flaked almonds
1 egg yolk
1 tablespoon water
icing sugar for dusting,
   optional

Place the raisins in a bowl with the rum and leave to macerate overnight.

Mix the yeast with the warm milk in a small bowl.

Combine the flour, sugar, salt and yeast mixture in the bowl of an electric mixer. Beat on medium speed with the dough hook. Add the eggs, one at a time, mixing well after each addition. Beat for about 5 minutes until the dough is smooth and elastic.

Turn the mixer speed to low and add the butter, bit by bit. Once it's all incorporated, increase the speed to medium again and beat for about 8 minutes until the dough comes away from the sides of the bowl. Briefly mix in the macerated raisins.

Transfer the dough to a bowl, cover with a clean tea towel and leave to rise at room temperature for about 2 hours.

Knock back the dough by punching it with your fists a few times. Roll it out to a rectangle and fold it onto itself to form a sausage shape.

Butter the kougelhopf mould with the extra butter and scatter the flaked almonds onto the sides and base of the mould. Place the dough into the mould, adjusting it gently to fit. Mix the egg yolk and water together to make eggwash and seal the ends together. Leave to rise in a warm place (something around 25°C is ideal) for another 2 hours.

Preheat the oven to 200°C. Bake the kougelhopf for 20 minutes then cover with baking paper and cook for a further 20 minutes. Remove the cake from the oven and place on a rack to cool. Turn out after about 15 minutes and leave to cool completely. Dust with icing sugar just before serving.

Serves 8–10

MACAROONS

Macarons

From the Paris Region by Pierrick Boyer

These delicious small, round cakes are crunchy on the outside and smooth and soft in the centre. They were made famous by the great Parisian pâtisserie, Ladurée, where every year a new flavour of macaroon is created. A little experience is required to make macaroons well, so you may need to make a few batches to perfect the technique.

50 ml water	160 g almond meal
150 g caster sugar	160 g icing sugar
120 g egg whites	160 g thickened cream
2 vanilla pods, seeds scraped	160 g dark cooking chocolate

Preheat the oven to 145°C. Line 2 baking sheets with baking paper.

Combine the sugar and water in a saucepan and bring to a simmer. Place a candy thermometer in the pan and cook until the syrup reaches 121°C.

Just before the syrup reaches temperature, place the remaining egg whites in an electric mixer and whisk to stiff peaks. With the motor running, slowly drizzle in the hot syrup. Continue whisking at a low speed for a few minutes.

In a mixing bowl, combine the remaining egg whites with the vanilla seeds, almond meal and icing sugar. Mix in a spoonful of the beaten egg whites to loosen the mixture. Then use a plastic scraper to mix in the remaining egg whites. Transfer the mixture to a piping bag fitted with a 1 cm nozzle.

Pipe small 3 cm mounds of the mixture onto the baking trays, spacing them evenly. Tap the trays lightly on the work surface to settle the mixture, then leave to rest for 1 hour.

Transfer to the oven and bake for 8–10 minutes.

Meanwhile, bring the cream to the boil. Pour the hot cream onto the cooking chocolate and stir until very smooth. Leave the chocolate to cool and firm up a little but don't allow it to set. Spoon into a piping bag.

Pipe neat dollops of chocolate onto the flat sides of half the macaroons. Top each with a macaroon and sandwich together. Store in an airtight container.

Makes 30–35 macaroons

RASPBERRY FRUIT JELLIES

Pâte de fruit aux framboises

From the Limousin Region by Philippe Mouchel

You find these exquisite, soft and flavoursome fruit jellies in the best French pâtisseries and they are often served with coffee in top restaurants.

Making these jellies requires some experience and you will need a few items of specialist equipment, such as a candy thermometer and a fruit jelly frame.

1.2 kg strained raspberry purée

1.1 kg caster sugar

30 g apple pectin

200 g liquid glucose

1 ½ tablespoon citric acid

2 tablespoons raspberry liqueur

200 g sugar

Line a tray with baking paper and place a 40 cm square fruit jelly frame on top.

Place the strained raspberry purée in a saucepan and bring to a simmer.

Mix 100 g of the caster sugar with the apple pectin and stir into the raspberry purée. Add the liquid glucose and the remaining sugar and bring to a slow boil.

Place a candy thermometer in the pan and cook until the syrup reaches 108°C. Stir from time to time and brush the edges of the pan with a little water if necessary, to keep them clean.

Dissolve the citric acid in the raspberry liqueur and add it to the purée once it reaches 108°C. Very carefully pour the jelly mixture into the frame and spread it evenly. Allow to cool, then refrigerate for at least 2 hours to set.

Gently remove the frame and cut the fruit jelly into 3 cm squares. Place the jellies onto a plate of sugar and coat delicately with sugar. Store in a dry cake tin in layers separated with baking paper.

Makes about 150 jellies

ALMOND AND HONEY NOUGAT

Nougat aux amandes et au miel
From the Provence-Rhône Region

Nougat is the speciality of the town of Montélimar at the northern border of Provence and this festive sweet is one of the thirteen traditional Provençal Christmas desserts.

It takes experience to make nougat as you need to be able to juggle timing and temperatures – and you must take care not to burn yourself with the hot honey and syrup. You will need a candy thermometer to ensure the syrup and honey reach the exact temperatures. The syrup should take longer to reach 150°C than the honey takes to reach 135°C.

500 g raw almonds (skins on)	120 ml water
100 g pistachio nuts, skins removed and roughly chopped	380 g caster sugar
	180 g liquid glucose
100 g hazelnuts, skins removed if possible	250 g honey
	2 large egg whites
6 sheets rice paper	a pinch of cream of tartar

Preheat the oven to 150°C. Line a roasting tray with baking paper. Line a 35 x 25 x 2–3 cm swiss roll tin with baking paper.

Place the almonds, pistachios and hazelnuts in the prepared roasting tray and dry roast in the oven for about 20 minutes. Remove the nuts from the oven and keep warm until ready to use.

Reduce the oven temperature to 100°C.

To make a syrup, combine the water, sugar and glucose in a saucepan and bring to the boil over a medium heat. Place a candy thermometer in the pan and cook until the syrup reaches 150°C.

At the same time, heat the honey in a second saucepan. Bring to the boil over a medium heat and cook to 135°C.

Just before the honey and syrup reach temperature, combine the egg whites and cream of tartar in an electric mixer and whisk to soft peaks. With the motor running, slowly drizzle in the honey. Then drizzle in the hot syrup. Continue whisking at a low speed for about 5 minutes. Fold the roasted nuts into the nougat.

Arrange 3 sheets of rice paper in the prepared swiss roll tin. Tip in the nougat mixture and smooth the surface with a wet metal spoon. Lay the remaining 3 sheets of rice paper on top and leave the nougat to cool before covering with plastic wrap. Refrigerate when cold.

Remove the plastic wrap and turn the nougat out onto a chopping board. Use a large knife to cut into 3.5 x 2.5 cm pieces. The nougat becomes softer at room temperature.

Makes about 100 pieces

INDEX

A

Agneau grillé avec ratatouille et tapenade 85
Almond
    Almond and honey nougat 144
    Almond cream 133
Alsatian sauerkraut 92
Apple
    Apple pie with Armagnac 124
    Apple tart flamed with Calvados 122
Apricot compote with almonds
    and Armagnac 96
Asparagus and goat's cheese tart 16

B

Bean
    Bean stew with Toulouse sausages 93
    Tarbais beans 86
Béarnaise sauce 74
Beef
    Beef and beer stew 84
    Beef Burgundy 82
    Beef fillet with truffles and foie gras 78
    Beef rib eye with red wine sauce and
        vegetable purée 79
    Eye fillet steak with béarnaise sauce 74
    Rib of beef with red wine sauce 80
    Roast beef fillet with French-style peas 76
Beurre blanc sauce 41
Blue eye and scallops with butter sauce 43
Boeuf Bourguignon 82
Bouillabaisse 6
Bresse chicken with morel mushrooms 53
Buckwheat pancakes from Brittany 21

C

Cabbage
    Sauerkraut 92
*Cabillaud et coquilles St Jacques
    au beurre blanc* 43
Cakes
    Cherry mousse cake 118
    Chestnut cake 114

    Chocolate concorde cake 110
    Kougelhopf gateau 140
    Macaroons 142
    Mont Blanc chestnut cakes 132
    Paris Brest gateau 134
    Puff pastry and almond cream cake 133
    Raspberry ice-cream cake with
        meringue 112
    Savoie sponge cake 138
    St Honoré cake 136
    Strawberry sponge cake 116
    Walnut cake 139
Canard aux cerises 62
Carbonnade de boeuf 84
Cassoulet 65
Cassoulet Toulousain 93
Charlotte aux cerises 118
Cheese
    Asparagus and goat's cheese tart 16
    Cheese soufflé 22
    Roquefort cheese salad 12
Cherry clafoutis 120
Chestnut cake 114
Chicken
    Bresse chicken with morel mushrooms 53
    Chicken and prawn casserole 54
    Chicken Burgundy 56
    Chicken casserole cooked in Riesling 58
    Chicken fricassée with artichokes 53
    Poached chicken with vegetables 55
    Roast poussin with French lentils 51
    Sautéed chicken with tarragon cream
        sauce and carrots 50
Chocolate
    Chocolate concorde cake 110
    Chocolate icing 114
Choux pastry 134
Civet de langouste 36
Clafoutis aux cerises 120
Cognac and glacé fruit ice-cream 105
*Compote d'abricots à l'Armagnac
    et aux amandes avec un yaourt de brebis* 96

Coq au vin · 56
Coquilles St Jacques à la Parisienne · 30
Côte de boeuf à la Bordelaise · 80
Côte de boeuf sauce au vin rouge
    purée de legumes · 79
Côtes de pork aux choux · 90
Country-style pâté with pistachios · 11
Coupe de pêches et de cerises au citron · 98
Crayfish
    Crayfish and potato salad · 9
    Crayfish à l'Armoricaine · 34
    Crayfish à la Pariesienne · 10
    Crayfish stew · 36
Crème pâtissière · 130
    Pralinée · 134
Custard · 101, 116, 118

D

Daube de canard · 64
Daurade rôtie au beurre de Montpellier · 39
Desserts
    Apple pie with Armagnac · 124
    Apple tart flamed with Calvados · 122
    Apricot compote · 96
    Cherry clafoutis · 120
    Cognac and glace fruit ice cream · 105
    Hazelnut meringue with
        chestnut cream and raspberries · 109
    Nougat ice cream with
        raspberry sauce · 106
    Peaches poached in sweet wine · 97
    Peach Melba · 100
    Poached peach and cherry coupe
        in a lemon syrup · 98
    Raspberry fruit jellies · 142
    Raspberry ice cream cake
        with meringue · 112
    Raspberry trifles · 101
    Summer fruit mousse · 102
Duck
    Cassoulet · 65
    Duck casserole in red wine · 64
    Grilled duck with sautéed potatoes
        and curly salad · 60
    Roast duck fillet with cherries · 2

E

Ecrevisses en chausson · 17
Eye fillet steak with béarnaise sauce · 74

F

Filet de boeuf aux truffes et foie gras · 78
Filet de perche sauce au Chablis et
    aux asperges · 40
Filets de rouget poêlé à la tapenade,
    salade de fenouil · 31
Fish
    Blue eye and scallops with butter sauce · 43
    Fish quenelles · 32
    Fish stew · 6
    John dory with a creamy seafood sauce · 43
    Marinated sardines · 7
    Pan-fried salmon with butter sauce · 41
    Perch fillet with asparagus
        and Chablis sauce · 40
    Poached trout with hollandaise sauce · 46
    Red mullet with tapenade and
        a fennel salad · 31
    Rich Basque fish stew · 37
    Roast snapper with Montpellier butter · 39
    Trout with pine nuts and capers · 38
Flan aux pruneaux et aux poires · 126
Foie gras · 78
French-style onion and anchovy pizza · 23

G

Galettes Bretonnes au Sarazin · 21
Galettes de pomme de terre,
    salade de roquefort aux noix · 12
Gâteau aux marrons · 114
Gâteau aux noix · 139
Gâteau concorde au chocolat · 110
Gâteau de Savoie · 138

Gâteau fraisier 116
Gâteau St. Honoré 136
Gigot de sept heures 89
Glace plombières au cognac 105
Gratin de blettes 26
Gratin d'ecrevisses 19
Gratin of yabbies 18
Grilled duck with sautéed potatoes
and curly salad 60
Grilled loin of lamb with
ratatouille and tapenade 85

H
Hazelnut meringue with chestnut cream
and raspberries 109
Hollandaise sauce 46

I
Ice-creams and sorbets
Cognac and glace fruit ice-cream 105
Nougat ice-cream with
raspberry sauce 106
Raspberry ice-cream cake 112
Raspberry sorbet 112
Icing 139
Chocolate 114

J
John dory with a creamy seafood sauce 44

K
Kougelhopf gateau 140

L
La choucroûte Alsacienne 92
Lamb
Grilled loin of lamb with ratatouille
and tapenade 85
Lamb casserole with green olives 88
Roast lamb with Tarbais beans 86
Slow-cooked leg of lamb 89
Langouste à la Parisienne 10
Langouste à l'Armoricaine 34

Lapin de Garenne aux champignons 71
Lapin à la moutarde de Dijon 70
Lapin aux poivrons et aux olives 68
Lapin aux pruneaux 67
Lentils, French 51

M
Macaroons 142
Marinated sardines 7
Meringues 112
Méringue aux noisettes et crème
de marrons avec framboises 109
Mont Blanc chestnut cakes 132
Montpellier butter 39
Moules gratinées aux epinards 20
Moules marinières 5
Mousse de fruits d'eté 102
Mussels
Mussel and saffron soup 4
Mussel gratin with spinach 20
Mussels cooked with white wine
and herbs 5

N
Nougat 144
Nougat aux amandes et au miel 144
Nougat glacé avec un coulis de framboises 106
Nougat ice-cream with raspberry sauce 106

P
Pancakes, buckwheat 21
Pan-fried pork cutlets with cabbage 90
Pan-fried salmon with butter sauce 41
Paris Brest gateau 134
Pastry 24
Choux pastry 134, 136
Sweet shortcrust pastry 128
Paté de campagne à la pistache 11
Pâte de fruit aux framboises 142
Peaches
Peaches poached in sweet wine 97
Peach Melba 100

Poached peach and cherry coupe in a
    lemon syrup 98
Pêches poêlées au vin doux 97
Peas, French-style 76
Perch fillet with asparagus and
    chablis sauce 40
Petits gâteaux Mont Blanc 132
Pissaladière 23
Pithiviers 133
Poached chicken with vegetables 55
Poached trout with hollandaise sauce 46
Poussin rôti aux lentilles du Puy 51
Pork
    Alsation sauerkraut 92
    Bean stew with Toulouse sausages 93
    Country-style pâté with pistachios 11
    Pan-fried pork cutlets with cabbage 90
Potage aux primeurs 2
Poule au pot 55
Poulet au Riesling 58
Poulet aux artichauts 53
Poulet aux gambas 54
Poulet de Bresse aux morilles 52
*Poulet sauté à la crème d'estragon
    et aux carottes* 50
Potato galettes with roquefort
    cheese salad 12
Prawn stock 34
Provençal vegetable bake 27
Puff pastry and almond cream cake 133
Prune and pear flan 126

Q
Quenelles de poisson 32
Quiche Lorraine 24

R
Rabbit
    Rabbit casserole with capsicum
      and olives 68
    Rabbit stew with prunes 67
    Rabbit with a Dijon mustard sauce 70

    Wild rabbit with mushrooms 71
Ragoût de mouton aux olives vertes 88
Raspberry
    Raspberry ice-cream cake
      with meringue 112
    Raspberry fruit jellies 142
    Raspberry sauce 100
    Raspberry sorbet 112
    Raspberry tartlets 130
    Raspberry trifles 101
    Summer fruit mousse 102
Ratatouille 85
Rib of beef with red wine sauce 80
Rich Basque fish stew 37
Roast beef fillet with French-style peas 76
Roast duck fillet with cherries 62
Roast lamb with Tarbais beans 86
Roast poussin with French lentils 51
Roast snapper with Montpellier butter 39
Roscovite salad with cauliflower
    and prawns 14
Rôti d'agneau aux haricots Tarbais 86
Rôti de boeuf et petits pois à la Française 76
Rum syrup 114

S
St Honoré cake 136
St Pierre sauce Normande 44
Salads
    Curly 60
    Crayfish and potato 9
    Fennel salad 31
    Roquefort cheese salad 12
    Roscovite salad with cauliflower
      and prawns 14
Salade de langouste aux pommes de terre 9
Salade Roscovite 14
Sardines à l'escabèche 7
Sauces
    Béarnaise 74
    Butter 43

Beurre blanc	41
Creamy seafood	44
Dijon mustard	70
Hollandaise	46
Raspberry	100
Red wine	79, 80
Tarragon cream	50
Sauerkraut	92
Saumon poelé au beurre blanc	41
Sautéed chicken with tarragon cream sauce and carrots	50
Savoie sponge cake	138
Scallops the Parisian way	30
Seafood	
Chicken and prawn casserole	54
Crayfish à la Pariesienne	10
Crayfish à l'Armoricaine	34
Crayfish and potato salad	9
Crayfish stew	36
Gratin of yabbies	18
John dory with a creamy seafood sauce	44
Mussel and Saffron Soup	4
Mussel gratin with spinach	20
Mussels cooked with white wine and herbs	5
Scallops the Parisian way	30
Yabbies in puff pastry	17
Silverbeet gratin	26
Slow-cooked leg of lamb	89
Soufflé au fromage	22
Soups	
Young vegetable	2
Mussel and saffron	4
Soupe de moules au saffron	4
Sorbet, raspberry	112
Strawberry sponge cake	116
Sweet shortcrust pastry	128
Syrup	116
Rum	114
T	
Tapenade	31, 85
Tarte aux asperges et au fromage de chèvre	16
Tarte aux pommes à l'Armagnac	124

Tarte aux pommes flambée au Calvados	122
Tartelettes aux framboises	130
Tarts, pies and pizzas	
Apple pie with Armagnac	124
Apple tart flamed with Calvados	122
Asparagus and goat's cheese tart	16
French-style onion and anchovy pizza	23
Prune and pear flan	126
Quiche Lorraine	24
Raspberry tartlets	130
Tian aux légumes Provençals	27
Toulouse sausages	65, 93
Tournedos sauce béarnaise	74
Trout with pine nuts and capers	38
Truite au bleu hollandaise	46
Truite Grenobloise	38
Ttoro	37
V	
Vacherin aux framboises	112
Vegetables	
Peas, French-style	76
Potato galettes	12
Potatoes sautéed	60
Provençal vegetable bake	27
Ratatouille	85
Silverbeet gratin	26
Verrine aux framboises	101
W	
Walnut cake	139
Wild rabbit with mushrooms	71
Y	
Yabbies	
Yabbies in puff pastry	17
Gratin of yabbies	18
Young vegetable soup	2

ACKNOWLEDGEMENTS

I wish to express my very special thanks to SBS, particularly Les Murray and Ken Shipp, for commissioning me to produce *Taste Le Tour* over the past five years.

I want to thank my wife, Angie Gaté, who took part in all aspects of the project.

I am very grateful to Peter Warren who helped produce the series.

Most of all, thanks to the French chefs, pastry chefs, friends and family members who have contributed recipes published in this book, especially Philippe Mouchel, Sebastian Buror, Pierrick Boyer, Stéphane Langlois, Elisabeth Kerdelhué, Angie Gaté and Michael Gaté.

Lastly, thanks to Hardie Grant's publishing team for making the experience of putting the book together so enjoyable.

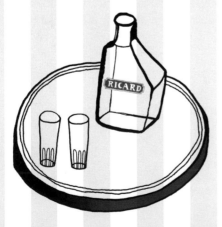